R.S. Prussia

The Art Nouveau Years

With hidden image patterns

Schiffer Publishing Ltd

4880 Lower Valley Road, Atglen, PA 19310 USA

Leland & Carol Marple

Designed by "Sue"
Typeset in Times New Roman

ISBN: 0-7643-0508-5
Printed in China
1 2 3 4

Published by Schiffer Publishing Ltd.
4880 Lower Valley Road
Atglen, PA 19310
Phone: (610) 593-1777; Fax: (610) 593-2002
E-mail: Schifferbk@aol.com
Please write for a free catalog.
This book may be purchased from the publisher.
Please include $3.95 for shipping.

Please try your bookstore first.

We are interested in hearing from authors
with book ideas on related subjects.

Contents

Acknowledgments

Trade catalog information has played a major part in our understanding and subsequent presentation of the products exported to the United States by the Reinhold Schlegelmilch Porcelain Factory. The acquisition of a substantial portion of the material for this book was made possible by the staff members at various libraries. We want to thank the following individuals for the retrieval and reproduction of archived records: Mr. Peter Rochon at the National Library of Canada; Ms. Carol Sandler at the Strong Museum Library; Mr. Tom Felt at the Library of Congress; and Ms. Patricia McCann at the University of New Mexico. We also want to thank Ms. Eleanor McD. Thompson at the Winterthur Library for helping us locate a source of Falker and Stern Co. catalogs. In addition, we want to thank Mr. Tom Gay for finding a long lost 1906 Falker and Stern Co. catalog, and Mr. Jim Kempster, who made us aware of the collection of decalcomanias from the German firm of C.A. Pocher, G.M.B.H., in the Strong Museum Library.

Examples of objects needed to show the diversity of china produced during the most popular part of the Art Nouveau movement were provided by several R.S. Prussia collectors and dealers. We want to thank the following for photographs from their collections: Mrs. Helen Bailey; Mrs. Rose Ellen Beyer; Mr. Dale Bowser; Mr. and Mrs. Harold Bragg; Mr. and Mrs. Terry Coy; Mr. and Mrs. Donald Diehl; Mr. and Mrs. Richard Elliott; Mr. and Mrs. Ron Fawcett; Dr. and Mrs. R.T. Faylona; Mr. and Mrs. Grady Hite; Mr. and Mrs. Paul Holsinger; Mr. and Mrs. Ken Jinde; Dr. and Mrs. Edward Johnson; Mr. and Mrs. Dennis Lemon; Mr. and Mrs. Edward Mott; Mr. David Mullins; Mrs. Dorothy Nance; Mr. and Mrs. Hank Schulken; Mr. and Mrs. Arlo Stender; Mr. and Mrs. Gordon Sweeter; Mr. and Mrs. Herman Thomas; Ms. Linda Van Gundy; Mr. and Mrs. David Van Norwick; Mr. and Mrs. Jack Williams; Ms. Judy White (J. White Antiques); and Mr. and Mrs. Jim Wroda.

This book would have been much more difficult to write (and would not have been as valuable a reference) if a new numbering system had to be used throughout. We want to thank Mary F. Gaston and her publisher (Collector Books, Paducah, KY) for permission to use the Steeple and RSP mold numbering systems revised by her in Series 3 and 4 of The Collector's Encyclopedia of R.S. Prussia.

Introduction

In our first book we describe the porcelain (china) products made up to the end of the nineteenth century for the American market by the Reinhold Schlegelmilch Porcelain Factory and Decorating Studio. Here, we continue the chronology of products by the illustration of china exported to America during the first of three consecutive, post-1900 periods. At the onset, the higher priced tableware purchased by domestic wholesale firms incorporated many Art Nouveau patterns. Apparently, Reinhold's products were well received, for the amount of R.S. Prussia in wholesale catalogs increased rapidly for several years[1]. This growth may have been due to the firm's technical expertise, allowing them to make thin, white china with deeply embossed floral motifs.

Reinhold's firm became recognized as one of the finest porcelain factories in Europe just as the Art Nouveau movement began to collapse. In spite of the launch of a new trademark and other changes in marketing strategy, R.S. Prussia listings in trade catalogs after 1905 show an accelerated year to year decline. By 1910, R.S.Prussia was largely replaced by china from other European or Japanese firms.

Our focus for this book is on the china introduced to the American market from 1900 through the Fall of 1904. During this short time, Reinhold's Suhl and Tillowitz factories began to make an amazing variety of novel products. Almost all strongly reflect the influence of the Art Nouveau movement. New types of scenic and portrait transfers allowed the creation of small works of art. Cobalt, gold, and other metallic colors were used to create brilliant effects. In addition, completely new lines of decorative products were introduced in response to the growing American market for luxury items.

Overall, we present the mold patterns for tableware products in chronological order. Chapter 1 begins with items made from early, pre-1900 molds, but decorated with printed transfers (decals). Essentially, this chapter begins where we stopped in *The Early Years*. The examples here show the slower transition in mold patterns compared to the turnover in decorating patterns. The bulk of this chapter is comprised of objects made from molds first offered in 1900, and decorated primarily with decals.

Mold patterns manufactured after 1900 are divided into two groups by the subject matter of the decals used for decoration. Mold patterns not normally decorated with the transfers used on the Hidden Image pattern are the subject of Chapter 2. Our goal is to represent the diversity of objects made and the transfers used for the decoration of each pattern without duplicating examples in other publications. In addition, we have made an attempt to be selective by showing the more collectible examples of each pattern[2]. Some entirely new patterns have been identified from trade catalog information. We have numbered these, and previously unnumbered patterns, by building upon the identification system developed by Mary F. Gaston (Gaston, 1994).

Chapter 3 provides a comprehensive presentation of the Hidden Image pattern. This ware is very popular today even though many collectors do not consider it to be part of R.S. Prussia. The longstanding and much debated question of origin is understandable in view of the rarity of marked examples. Fortunately, many Hidden Image items are illustrated in the Fall 1903 Falker and Stern Co. catalog, and all are described as Schlegelmilch products. A wide variety of objects in this pattern exist, far more than illustrated in all of the known sources combined. Based on the extended period of sale and the number of different objects made, the Hidden Image pattern was very likely the most commercially successful of all R.S. Prussia patterns.

Chapter 3 concludes with examples of R.S. Prussia tableware molds decorated (primarily) with the floral transfers used to decorate Hidden Image ware. Most of these molds are illustrated and/or described as Schlegelmilch products in trade catalogs printed between 1900 and 1905. While some were used to make both trade named[3] and trademarked merchandise, most patterns appear not to have been marked in any way. This has been a source of confusion for collectors, and has misled some to propose the involvement of other manufacturers and/or decorators. We explain why trade names became necessary, and show how just a few of these patterns were used for trade name products.

Chapter 4 is an in-depth presentation of the decorative products primarily marketed under the Royal Vienna Germany trade name. Decorative objects made by Reinhold Schlegelmilch prior to 1900 appear to have been a very small part of the overall production. We suspect the success of the firm's local competitor, Erdmann Schlegelmilch, in selling "inexpensive imitations" of Royal Vienna products (during 1899-1900) was a major factor in the decision to market luxury items.

This book also includes several Appendices we believe will be useful to those individuals seeking detailed information about R.S. Prussia. We also include indices for illustrations of objects marked with trade names, and for illustrations of scenic and portrait transfers.

Some of the R.S. Prussia patterns illustrated in Chapters 2-4 are shown in other books, but their inclusion was presented with the caveat they may not actually be products of Reinhold's firm! Part of this uncertainty develops when working with a limited number of objects. In addition, the absence of trade catalog data would have made it very difficult to recognize the role played by trade names. We also find that segregating R.S. Prussia by mark and/or trademark inhibits recognition of the continuity in R.S. Prussia products. Our documentation of R.S. Prussia, both by overlapping mold and transfer patterns and by trade literature, has allowed us to put the majority of Reinhold's American export products into a reasonably accurate chronological sequence. Our goal for this book is to fully document and illustrate the major products made during the rise in popularity of the Art Nouveau movement.

Endnotes

1. In the absence of financial information after 1901, B. Hartwich assumed the production by Reinhold Schlegelmilch peaked in 1897. Based on the extent of R.S. Prussia entries in the catalogs of wholesale firms such as Butler Bros. (who alone likely sold more merchandise than all the factory representatives combined), we believe production peaked about 1904.
2. While we would like to think otherwise, it is clear not all R.S. Prussia is avidly sought by collectors.
3. We use trade names for marks (logos) that either do not incorporate a direct reference to the manufacturer, or are not registered in the Coburg Ceramic Directory.

Values

Establishing values for objects shown in the illustrations was the only part of the preparation of this book to involve a significant level of uncertainty. Even though we had considerable input from collectors and several specialized china dealers, it has been an extraordinary challenge to keep the relative valuations of different types of objects within realistic limits. Unfortunately, even though R.S. Prussia from this period is offered at specialized auctions, lists of prices realized are of very limited use. The condition of lots is not always described, and yet the price realized normally reflects the degree of wear, number of small chips, and internal problems such as fractures and repairs. On the other hand, auction prices best define the relative valuations of objects with floral, scenic, and portrait transfer decorations. Lists of prices realized are often available from reputable auction firms.

Since most of the R.S. Prussia from this period was imported in large quantities through wholesale firms, virtually no products fall into the "rare" category. Consequently, we do not use the term "rare" in captions unless for some reason we suspect fewer than a half dozen objects exist in American collections. High prices do not necessarily accompany rare objects. Many collectors are reluctant to purchase a product not known to exist in another collection, and often fear these rarities are not factory products. We expect this situation to change once the full range of products made by Reinhold's factory is more widely known.

In general, there is a strong demand for post-1900 objects in cobalt, red, and lavender background colors, especially when combined with the copious use of gold. Portrait decorated items, especially with cobalt, bronze moire, or Royal Vienna (green/red) background colors, are also in strong demand when in excellent condition. Prices for floral decorated objects depend more on background color and the amount and type(s) of gold applied. Unlike pre-1900 ware, the premium for marked objects is not nearly so significant.

Regional differences strongly affect both the availability and price of R.S. Prussia. We find prices for equivalent items are much higher in the midwest than on either coast, often by a factor of two or more. This variation was exceptionally difficult to merge into the quoted price ranges, as they increase in steps of 50% or less. Up to $2,500, we put the value of objects into fixed price ranges. Generally, items valued above $2,500 are noted by $2,500+. There is no way to be more specific about the value of objects at higher price levels, for they are rarely offered for sale.

As is common for price guides, the quoted values are for objects in excellent condition. The price (and description) for a complete set is given in the captions. An item with obvious wear to the gold decoration, or to the transfer, should be substantially less than indicated. Objects with more serious problems such as chips, hairline fractures, or repairs should be considerably less than quoted. On occasion, some pieces may be offered or purchased well outside either end of the stated ranges. Neither the Author nor the Publisher assumes any responsibility for any losses incurred as a result of using this guide.

Chapter One
Transition Mold patterns

In our previous book we pictured objects made from molds we knew to have been used up to the beginning of 1900. Included was a series of "A" molds, for which we lacked extensive documentation. New information (see Appendix 1) has provided additional confirmation for their origin. With few exceptions, objects in both the "A" and "OM" series of molds were decorated by the outline transfer process[1]. However, about 1900, significant changes began to be made in the decoration of R.S. Prussia. The white or pastel colored backgrounds were replaced by intense colors, including cobalt, gold, and a unique peacock blue. Even more noticeable was the conversion from outline transfer patterns to printed, full color mineral transfers (called decalcomanias, or decals). The illustrations in trade catalogs clearly show this conversion was completed by 1902[2].

The change in type of decoration on R.S. Prussia had two major consequences. First, many of the early mold patterns were decorated with decals if not retired by 1900. Examples of this type are not plentiful, but there are a sufficient number to show the deliberate use of new decorations on salable mold patterns. Second, mold patterns making their debut in 1900 or 1901 were decorated with both types of transfers. Up to now, these transition molds have been largely ignored, or not recognized at all as part of R.S.Prussia.

We begin Chapter 1 by showing objects in the "OM" series of molds shown in Chapter 6 in *The Early Years*, but decorated with new types of transfers. This section is followed by patterns first appearing in 1900 or 1901, and decorated with both types of transfers. All of these post-1900 patterns are primarily decorated with decals rather than outline transfers, although this might not be reflected by the examples shown here.

The molds decorated with small transfer patterns shown in Chapter 7 of *The Early Years* were also used for a few years after 1900. We conclude Chapter 1 with decal decorated examples of these pre-1900 patterns. We know of no new molds appearing after 1900 to be decorated with both small outline transfers and large decals.

We have not found the printed transfers used on the objects in this chapter to be systematically named or numbered elsewhere. Where applicable, we describe transfers by the code used previously. Transfers described with Hidden Image numbers are cross-referenced in Index 1 to examples in Chapters 2 and 3. We continue with the assignment of OM numbers to new transition mold patterns so there is a continuity of presentation. When available, marked or trademarked objects are shown before other examples. The figure caption

for each object provides the base color, mold and transfer pattern identification, and the overall size. Any special features of the object are noted in the caption. For some patterns, additional information is available. We discuss this next, rather than in the corresponding captions.

A strong influence of the Art Nouveau movement can be seen in the new patterns produced for 1900. The symmetrical elements in the molds from earlier years start to disappear. In their place are leaf and flower patterns taken directly from nature. In addition, there seems to have been a purposeful modification in the individual pattern elements to accommodate the application to objects of varying sizes. Mold OM 75 provides a case in point. Each item exhibits a slightly different flower shape, or a different number of flowers. However, the relative placement of leaves, flowers, scrolls and other elements is unchanged. A pleasing effect is achieved when different pieces are in use, for the boredom of identical patterns is replaced by an interesting variation on a theme. We show a large number of objects in this mold, as it was one of two major patterns for 1900.

The "Oxford" (RSP Mold 706) is a pattern name we first see in the Fall 1900 G. Sommers & Co. wholesale catalog. This pattern is easily remembered by the ear shaped handles and pierced feet. Even though the mold continued to be produced through 1905, objects with floral decoration are uncommon. Many of the objects we have examined in this mold have internal fractures. We are able to illustrate a few objects decorated with the "Italian Head" decoration[3] carried by Butler Bros. near the end of the production run. Overall, objects in this pattern are scarce, even though they were carried by several large wholesale firms.

Pattern OM 80 was carried by Falker and Stern Co. in the Spring of 1901. Generally, patterns in spring catalogs are those not sold out the previous holiday season. Consequently, OM 80 was undoubtedly first made in 1900. Interestingly, this is the first pattern known to be used for the Saxe Altenburg Germany trade name products. We will return to a discussion of the origin for this and other trade names in Chapter 3.

Only two small transfer molds, OM 120 and OM 140 (clamshell), continued to be produced beyond 1900. Of these, mold OM 140 appears more frequently in trade catalogs. With the exception of the "Italian Head" decoration, other decorating patterns used on this mold are almost unique. Apparently, production of OM 140 continued into 1905 as examples are known to be trademarked with the classic RS Prussia Wreath.

After examining long runs of trade catalogs, we note most mold patterns were produced for only two to three years. We suspect few R.S. Prussia mold patterns sold well enough to last longer.[4] In retrospect, a fresh, new appearance for each year must have been essential to a business where most products were eventually purchased as gifts.

Endnotes

1. Some of the products from the early 1890s seem to have been completely hand decorated.

2. Although illustrations of china in all trade catalogs up through 1904 were done by artists working from production samples, the quality of artwork allows us to clearly distinguish between an outline transfer and a printed decal.

3. The portraits in this series are designated "Tillie", "Litta", and "Flossie" by George Terrell, Jr. (Terrell, 1982).

4. Toy tea sets, shaving mugs, and cup/saucer sets were frequently carried for many years. A variety of transfer types and subjects may be found on these longer lived patterns.

Plate 1. Cup/saucer set, white, Mold A1, (King George Pattern), printed decor used after 1905, cup 2.5" h, saucer 5" d. Under $50.

Plate 2. Individual berry bowl, green edge, Mold OM 5, decor HI 2, 5" w. Under $25.

Plate 3. Relish tray, buff/green edge, Mold OM 13, decor HI 4, 11.25" l. Under $50.

Plate 4. Salad bowl, cobalt edge, Mold OM 40, decor P4, 11.5" d. $250-400.

Plate 6. Plate, green edge, Mold OM 47, small rose decor, 7.5" d. Under $50.

Plate 7. Cream/sugar set, Mold OM 47, pink/white aster decor, pitcher 2.25" h., sugar 1.5" h. Under $50.

Plate 5. Dresser tray, green edge, Mold OM 44, decor HI 10, 11.25" l. $75-100.

Plate 8. Biscuit jar, white, Mold OM 47 (finial damaged), multi-color transfer, 7" h. $150-$250.

9

Plate 9. Cake plate, green/white, Mold OM 48, decor P 2, 11" d. $150-$250.

Plate 11. Salad bowl, rust color rim, Mold OM 49, decor pink/yellow roses, 10" d. $150-$250.

Plate 10. Cake plate, cobalt/white, Mold OM 48, decor FD M, 12" d. $250-$400.

Plate 12. Dresser tray, green/tan edge, Mold OM 57, decor HI 1, 11.75" w. $100-$150.

Plate 13. Spoon holder, white, Mold OM 61, decor HI 13, 4" h. Under $50.

Plate 14. Chocolate pot, 2 cup/saucer sets, Mold OM 62, decor FD P, pot 9" h., cups 3" h., saucers 4" d. $400-$600.

Plate 15. Mustard pot, pink/tan top edge, Mold OM 62, decor HI 7, 3.5" h. $75-$100.

Plate 17. Cake plate, red/white edge, Mold OM 69, decor P 4, 10.25" d. $250-$400.

Plate 18. Cake plate, dusty rose edge, Mold OM 69, courting scene-lady in yellow dress, 9.5" d. $150-$250.

Plate 16. Cake plate, cobalt edge, Mold OM 69, decor P 4, 10.25" d. $250-$400.

Plate 19. Cake plate, burnt orange edge, Mold OM 69, decor P 4, 11"
d. $100-$150.

Plate 20. Small tray, green, Mold OM 72, decor P 4, 8.75" x 5.5".
Under $50.

Plate 22. Salad bowl, red/buff edge, Mold OM 73, decor P 4, 9" d.
$100-$150.

Plate 23. Cake plate, red/buff edge, Mold OM 73, decor not numbered, 11.75" d. $150-$250.

Plate 21. Salad bowl with handle, Mold
OM 73, decor P 4, 11" d. $400-$600.

Plate 24. Salad bowl, buff spokes, Mold OM 73, 10" d. $250-$400.

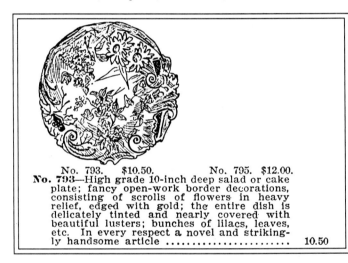

No. 793. $10.50.   No. 795. $12.00.
No. 793—High grade 10-inch deep salad or cake plate; fancy open-work border decorations, consisting of scrolls of flowers in heavy relief, edged with gold; the entire dish is delicately tinted and nearly covered with beautiful lusters; bunches of lilacs, leaves, etc. In every respect a novel and strikingly handsome article 10.50

Plate 25. Catalog illustration of Mold OM 75 (Harvest mold), 10" cake plate shown in G. Sommers & Co. Fall 1900 catalog. *Courtesy of Minnesota Historical Society Library.*

Plate 27. Cake plate, cobalt/white edge, Mold OM 75, decor P 4, 12" d. $250-$400.

Plate 28. Cake plate, rust edge, Mold OM 75, decor P 4, 9.5" d. $100-$150.

Plate 26. Bread tray, cobalt/white, Mold OM 75, decor HI 10, 12.5" w. Marked RS Steeple Germany (blue). $250-$400.

Plate 29. Cake plate, pink edge, Mold OM 75, decor OT 27, 10" d. $100-$150.

Plate 31. Salad bowl, blue/white edge, heart shape Mold OM 75, decor P 4, 10.5" d. Very scarce shape. $250-$400.

Plate 30. Cake plate, yellow edge, Mold OM 75, decor P 2, 9.25" d. $100-$150.

Plate 32. Salad bowl, green/buff edge, Mold OM 75, decor P 4, 9" d. $75-$100.

Plate 33. Celery tray, blue edge, Mold OM 75, decor P 4, 13.5" long. Marked "Royal Coburg" in black script. $100-$150.

Plate 34. Small relish tray, buff edge, Mold OM 75, decor OT 44, 8.5" l. $75-$100.

Right: Plate 37. Chocolate pot, blue edge, Mold OM 75, decor P 4, 9.25" h. $150-$250.

Plate 35. Dresser tray, green edge, Mold OM 75, decor not numbered, 12" l. $100-$150.

Plate 38. Tooth-pick holder, green underglaze, Mold OM 75, decor P3, 2.25" h. $75-$100.

Plate 36. Demitasse set, blue edges, Mold OM 75, decor P 4, pot 6.75" h., cream 3.25" h., sugar 3.5" h. $250-$400.

Right: Plate 39. Biscuit jar, pink edge, Mold OM 75, decor P 4, 8" h. $150-$250.

15

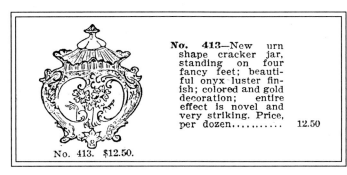

Plate 40. Catalog illustration of #413 cracker jar in RSP Mold 706 from the G. Sommers & Co. Fall 1900 wholesale catalog. Based on other objects in this mold, the decor as shown is completely hand painted. *Courtesy of Minnesota Historical Society Library.*

Plate 43. Chocolate pot, green/pink on buff, Mold RSP 706, "Countess Litta" Italian head decor, 8.75" h. $600-$900.

Plate 41. Sugar bowl, blue/buff on white, Mold RSP 706, decor ST-8, 5.5" h. $50-$75.

Plate 44. Tea cup, purple/buff, Mold RSP 706, "Tillie" Italian head decor, 2.25" h. Under $50.

Plate 42. Sugar bowl, blue/buff on white, Mold RSP 706, "Countess Litta" Italian head decor, 5.5" h. $75-$100.

Plate 45. Cracker jar, green/pink on buff, Mold RSP 706, "Flossie" Italian head decor, 7" h. $900-1300.

Plate 48. Salad bowl, beige, Mold OM 79 (Lyre mold), decor P2, 10.5" d. $150-$250.

Plate 46. Cracker jar, green/pink on buff, Mold RSP 706, "Countess Litta" Italian head decor, 7" h. $900-$1300.

Plate 49. Salad bowl, green/buff, Mold OM 79, decor OT 27, 10.5" d. $150-$250.

Plate 47. Catalog illustration of #1509 salad bowl in Mold OM 79 from the G. Sommers & Co. Holiday issue of 1902. This same bowl was also offered as #849 in the Holiday issue for 1900 by the same firm. *Courtesy of Minnesota Historical Society Library.*

M 1509. $9.00.

M 1509—Large, extra deep bowl, in leaf shape; heavily corrugated edges; 11 inches; rich gold and luster decorations; beautiful sprays of daisies.................................... 9.00

Plate 50. Salad bowl, green/buff edge, Mold OM 79, decor HI 7, 10.5" d. $150-$250

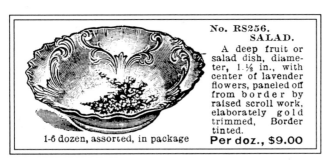

No. RS256.
SALAD.
A deep fruit or salad dish, diameter, 1.½ in., with center of lavender flowers, paneled off from border by raised scroll work, elaborately gold trimmed, Border tinted.
1-6 dozen, assorted, in package
Per doz., $9.00

Plate 51. Illustration of #RS256 deep fruit or salad dish in Mold OM 80 from the Spring 1901 Falker and Stern Co. catalog. *Courtesy of Amador Collections, Rio Grande Historical Collections, New Mexico State University Library.*

Plate 53. Salad bowl, green/buff, Mold OM 80, decor OT 31A, 10.5" d. $150-$250.

Plate 54. Salad bowl, green rim with metallic trim, Mold OM 80, decor HI 5, 10.5" d. $150-$250.

Plate 52. Salad bowl, cobalt rim, Mold OM 80, decor P 4, 10.5" d. $250-$400

Plate 58. Celery vase, white, Mold OM 120, multi-flower decal, 6.5" h. $75-$100.

Plate 55. Cup/saucer set, bright yellow with pink rose transfer, Mold OM 133 variation, cup 2" h., tray 5.25" w. $100-$150.

Plate 56. Teapot, pink stripe with small rose decor, Mold OM 120, 5.5" h. $100-$150.

Plate 59. Salad bowl, pink/blue edge, Mold OM 140, "Countess Litta" Italian head decor, 10" d. $250-$400.

Plate 57. Chocolate pot, Mold OM 120, OT flowers, spider web decal in swirls, 8.5" h. $100-$150.

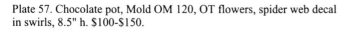

Plate 60. Cake plate, turquoise with white center, Mold OM 140, decor not numbered, 11.5" d. $100-$150.

19

Plate 61. Salad bowl, purple edge, Mold OM 140, orange poppies and white daisies, 9" d. $75-$100.

Plate 62. Individual cake plate, blue/buff, Mold OM 140, "Flossie" Italian head decor, 7.5" d. $75-$100.

Plate 63. Salad bowl, light green/buff, Mold OM 140, decor FD 47, 9.75" d. $100-$150.

Plate 64. Toothpick, magenta top, Mold OM 140, P 6 decor, 2" h. $75-$100.

Plate 65. Cream pitcher, lime green, Mold OM 152, "Queen Louise" decor, 3.25" h. $75-$100.

Plate 66. Mustard pot, white, Mold OM 150A, large pink rose decal, 2.5" h. $50-$75.

Plate 68. Vase, cobalt top, no mold number, large transfer P 1, 8.75" h. $250-$400.

Plate 67. Vase, red top, no mold number, transfer OT 31, 4.5" h. Marked RS Steeple Germany (gold). $250-$400.

Chapter Two
Post-1900 Mold Patterns

The illustrations in Chapter 2 are of objects made from mold patterns first sold in America from 1900 through 1904. For the most part, they are arranged year-to-year in order of their appearance in trade catalogs. There are a few undocumented patterns, and they are positioned according to the type of decoration associated with them. Several of the patterns illustrated here continued to be made after 1905. Trademarked objects in these patterns identify them as R.S. Prussia products. As we have noted before, only part of the total inventory of mold and transfer patterns were phased out each year by Reinhold's firm. Objects made after 1905 overlap the use of the classic R.S. Prussia Wreath (1905-1910), and may be so marked. In addition, the identification of many other patterns is made possible by the descriptions in trade catalogs.

Falker and Stern Co. trade catalogs provide the best single reference for post-1900 R.S. Prussia patterns. This firm began to carry R.S. Prussia in 1898, a full ten years after the start up of their business. Many pre-1900 mold patterns were named, a practice common to contemporary wholesale firms. Beginning in 1900, Falker and Stern Co. included the manufacturers initials as part of the catalog order number. Both "RS" and "ST" (Suhl and Tillowitz) were used for objects from Reinhold's factories. Other frequent listings include "K" (possibly for Reinhold's major competitor, Bauer, Rosenthal & Co. located at Kronach, Bavaria), "L" (unknown manufacturer), "OS" for Oscar Schlegelimlch, and "ES" for Erdmann Schlegelmilch[1]. This system was partially replaced in 1903, using "K" as a prefix regardless of the source. However, after the Spring issue of 1903, the Schlegelmilch origin was listed in individual catalog descriptions[2].

Some of the patterns first manufactured after 1900 have not always been considered to be part of R.S. Prussia. Part of the reason for this is the infrequent use of either recognizable trade names or trademarks. For various reasons, some of these patterns seem to be scarce, even though they were carried by more than one wholesale firm. As a result, they have not been shown in earlier publications. For those molds in Chapter 2 adequately characterized in other publications, we provide a few objects to show the pattern elements. Where choice permitted, we selected the more collectible decorations for each pattern. Unfortunately, examples and/or references to a few documented patterns could not be found. We include trade catalog descriptions for these patterns so collectors have additional source material for the identification of R.S. Prussia.

The order of mold presentation closely follows the first year of appearance in the trade literature. New mold patterns, or patterns not otherwise designated, are numbered with an "RS" prefix. Most patterns are prefaced with an illustration from a trade catalog, and the corresponding caption notes additional firms to carry the pattern and the known years of sale. The trade name or trademark on the objects following are stated at the end of the description in the corresponding captions. Additional information is available for some patterns, and we include it here rather than in the captions.

The scarcity today of objects in cobalt colors is partially due to the very high wholesale price for items with this decoration. For example, the "Royal Prussian" salad bowl #863 in Mold RS 1 was offered 1900-1901 by G. Sommers & Co. for $2 each. This is almost twice the price of R.S. Prussia bowls with other decorations. Although we do not illustrate this item, the bowl utilizes a new type of cobalt decoration where the cobalt shades from dark to light. The coloration is identical to the example of Mold RS 2 illustrated in Plate 72. Up to this time, embossed mold designs were highlighted in cobalt, or the cobalt colorant was applied heavily to segments defined by the decorating pattern. The type of cobalt coloration most desired by collectors today is different yet, and appears on china produced after 1902.

RSP Mold 502 (also RSP Mold 560), commonly called the Morning Glory mold, was first introduced in 1900, and was still being sold by wholesale firms in 1904. Each object, including the lid, is made in the shape of a flower. The only exception we know of is the lid to the covered butter. Floral transfers were commonly used for decoration. The series of "Italian Head"[3] portrait transfers is first shown in 1903. We include a sufficient number of examples to characterize many of the floral transfers, as they are found on very few other R.S. Prussia patterns. We are fortunate to be able to show an example (partial) of the tête-à-tête set, comprised of a pot, 2 cup/saucers, cream/sugar, and tray[4]. The pieces to this set are all quite small, and without the tray, can be easily mistaken for a toy tea set[5].

RSP Mold 256 (also RSP Mold 451) is a pattern carried by Falker and Stern Co. (1901-1903) and Butler Bros. (1903). We do not show examples decorated with the fruit transfer and glass silhouette, for these were later products. This series of jug, wine glass, and pitcher silhouettes (on a different mold) was carried by Butler Bros. in 1905. RSP Mold 256, along with RSP Mold 343, was a workhorse pattern, for production is known to have continued past 1910.

Mold RS 6 is another mold pattern first seen in 1902 trade catalogs. This mold incorporates a complex handle into upright objects. While difficult to see from the illustrations, the bottom part of the handle veers to the left as it enters the body. This irregularity allows one to easily differentiate the old from reproduction mugs, for in the latter, the handle lies completely in one plane. We know of no marked objects in this mold.

New patterns for 1902 include the very scarce Mold RS 3, or "Tulip" pattern. This mold is one of the very few to be decorated with a gold center medallion. We originally thought this pattern to be of Austrian origin until we found the Schlegelmilch designation in a Falker and Stern Co. catalog. We have recorded few types of objects in the Tulip pattern in the last few years, although a wide variety were carried by wholesale firms.

The "Roman" pattern, a name used by G. Sommers & Co. for containers (biscuits, chocolate pots, and cream/sugar sets), is currently known as RSP Mold 621. This is one of the few molds to have the lid extend over the top of the rim. Nearly all R.S. Prussia lids fit within the rim, fitting equally well upside down as right side up. Undoubtedly, this characteristic allowed the lids to be packed upside down on the pot in order to protect the finial during shipment.

Objects made in RSP Mold 703 are frequently confused with those made in RSP Mold 10, owing to the use of Lily of the Valley decoration. There are, however, no embossed flowers in the design of Mold 703. No bowls in Mold 703 are shown here, but they were made[6]. Their shape is similar to bowls in Mold RS 7.

Few molds seem to be as scarce as Mold RS 5, the "Panel Pansy" mold, even though it too was carried by several wholesale firms for several years. Containers in this mold are easily recognized by the complex, irregularly shaped handle. Here also, this feature does not show well in the illustrations.

Mold RS 7 is distinguished by embossed cattails extending from the leaf section. This leaf pattern seems to have been used only for various types of plates and bowls. The pattern is not identical to the "Ivy Base" pattern, Mold RS 18, used mainly for upright objects. Bowls decorated with the "Italian Head" series of portraits are known, and are illustrated by Barlock (Barlock and Barlock, 1976). This mold may have been updated in 1905 by a version with larger, segmented leaves and no cattails. We do not know of any trade name or trademark on this mold except for "Royal Oldenburg" in red block letters (Capers mark RS 5.3R 9).

In the Fall of 1903, Falker and Stern Co. illustrate both a combination candlestick and pin box, and a combination candlestick and matchsafe. The use of the "RS" prefix in the inventory number indicates these items had been in stock in prior years. Unfortunately, we have not been able to find complete examples of these items for illustration here.

The children's toy tea set HD 6883, offered in the Spring 1902 G. Sommers & Co. catalog, was in production for at least eight years. We illustrate two examples, one with fruit decor (used on R.S. Prussia tableware from 1905-1908), and one with hand painted designs. We have found hand painted versions of these small sets to have been made as late as 1906. This mold was also decorated with "Eskimo figures and polar animals"[7], and sold by Butler Bros. as a September special in 1911.

We include in this segment the Bowtie mold, RSP Mold 504, even though we cannot document a date of manufacture from trade catalogs. Our decision was based on the pre-1905 type of decoration used on most objects in this mold pattern. We suspect the bowtie pattern was primarily sold between 1903 and 1906, as some examples are known to be marked with the classic RS Prussia Wreath.

Two other molds we have found to be easily confused are RSP Mold 571, and Mold RS 9. The different shapes of the salad bowl in these two molds is clearly illustrated in a Nov. 1903 Butler Bros. catalog. The proper assignment of objects to these molds has also been a challenge. We had several cup and saucer sets in RSP Mold 571 for over a year before we identified the pattern. The cup/saucer set in Mold RS 9 were mystery pieces until we obtained a photograph of the cake plate. The cake plate and cup/saucer set in mold RS 9 are both illustrated in the Nov. 1903 Butler Bros. catalog.

Surviving examples of Mold RS 8, a new pattern for 1903, are very scarce. Were it not for the fact that we had access to a collection of chocolate pots, we would not have a suitable object to illustrate this pattern.

RS Steeple Mold 5 is very similar to RS Steeple Molds 10 or 15 (10 and 15 are identical patterns). The major distinction of Mold 5 is the "arrow" in the rim pointing toward the center. In addition, we know of no containers made from Mold 5, and none appear in 1903-1906 trade catalogs. It is not unusual to find objects from both Molds 5 and 10 decorated exactly the same, because they were contemporary molds.

For years, the two body shapes of RS Steeple Mold 2 were a puzzle to us. From the front, the shapes are virtually identical. When viewed from the back, the foot of one is almost round, but the foot of the other is hexagonal. Illustrations in the 1903 Webb-Freyschlag catalog show both of these versions to have been made at exactly the same time. The hexagon shaped bowl was used for the "Art Design", decorated with a scenic transfer and finished with the new peacock blue and green iridescent tints. At $2 each, these were almost as expensive as bowls with perforated edges shown in Chapter 3.

Examples of RS Steeple Molds 10 and 15 are grouped together under RS Steeple Mold 10. Objects in many different decorations were carried by Butler Bros. and Webb-Freyschlag, but not in the cobalt colors illustrated here. Items decorated "in rich effect", with solid gold and floral transfers sold for more than twice the price of examples tinted with ivory and blended green. While R.S. Prussia items with cobalt decor were not generally carried by wholesale firms, where they are listed, they are far more expensive than any other color. Most cobalt items in this mold pattern are marked with the RS Steeple Germany (red) trademark, though other trade names are known[8].

Many types of objects in RS Steeple Mold 7 are known to have been made. While not common, bowls made in RS Steeple Mold 7 are found with perforated edges. We are fortunate in having two examples to show here. The bread and milk set (or mush set), always included an underplate. Few complete mush sets in any of the R.S. Prussia patterns seem to have survived intact.

The pattern shown here as Mold RS 10 was previously included with the Modified Iris pattern, RS Steeple Mold 6[9]. We have made a distinction between the two patterns, for bowls in the Modified Iris pattern are very common, but bowls in pattern RS 10 are very scarce.

RS Steeple Mold 26 was a pattern carried by many wholesale firms in a variety of shapes and decorations. Although we have tried to avoid illustrating rarities unavailable to collectors, we do show one example of the "Nymph" decoration. This example may have been sent here as a sample, or it may have been originally sold in England and later brought to this country. The transfer is one of a set of two, and may be found in the collection of decals from the firm of C.A. Pocher, G.M.B.H. (See Appendix 3.)

The pattern designated as Mold RS 11 is easily distinguished from RS Steeple Mold 10 by the arrows below the floral rim segments. This same attribute allows the distinction from RSP Mold 91, a mold produced between 1906 and 1908. The distinction from RSP Mold 82 (Point and Clover), also first produced in 1906, is provided by the absence of embossed ovals in the rim between the floral segments.

The "Chestnut" or "Buckeye" pattern has already been assigned two mold numbers, RSP Mold 347 and RSP Mold 657. We think it less confusing to use a single number for each pattern, so we arbitrarily use RSP Mold 347 for the examples shown here. Some objects in this pattern when decorated with "water and sky effect with flowers and swans" may be marked with a gold "Royal Berlin" and star[10]. A cracker jar with this hand painted, transfer outline decor is illustrated in the Fall 1904 Butler Bros. catalog (R1098), so it is very likely this firm distributed, among others, Royal Berlin trade named merchandise.

Four mold patterns, RS 13, RS 14, RS 15, and RS 16 are illustrated in the Nov. 1903 Falker and Stern Co. catalog. Of these, we have been able to locate only one object in Mold RS 13. We show this object here, rather than in Chapter 4, even though it is marked with a gold "Royal Vienna Germany."

Cup and saucer sets were a staple product line for most wholesale firms. Catalogs distributed as early as 1895 show page after page of all shapes of mugs, and many sizes of cup/saucer sets. The Nov. 1903 and Fall 1904 Butler Bros. trade catalogs show a large selection of after dinner (demitasse) sets, now identifiable as R.S. Prussia. Often, these sets were sold in combinations of three styles such as the "Venetian" assortment, with raised gold and tint decorations in Venetian effect. Most were sold at a half dozen to a package, as shipped directly from the manufacturer. When two of an assortment are illustrated, the identification of one by trademark allows for the identification of the other. Associations of this type, as well as through transfers, provide a high level of confidence in the R.S. origin of the demitasse sets illustrated here.

R.S. Prussia boxes or bon bons are, categorically, very scarce. Here also, the illustration of two shapes, sold in a combination of three, allows us to deduce the R.S. origin for one if the other is known. The origin of some of the boxes shown in the Nov. 1903 Falker and Stern Co. trade catalog is indicated from the inventory number. However, we could not find examples of them for illustration.

Beginning in 1903, we see many different types of trays in trade catalogs. Butler Bros. offered five assortments containing either three (large) or six different (small) shapes. Fortunately, two shapes are illustrated from each group. Just as for boxes, sequential comparisons have allowed us to identify many new shapes of R.S. Prussia trays.

Toy tea sets continued to be popular in 1903, and many wholesale firms provided a large selection[11]. Better R.S. Prussia sets frequently contained 15, 17, or 21 pieces, with and without spoons, all in a lined box. The "extra size" 23 piece toy tea sets were often described as "almost large enough for after dinners", or "large enough for actual use". Webb-Freyschlag offered several child's tête-à-tête sets (from unknown manufacturers) where the pots were shaped more like chocolate pots than tea pots. Consequently, there appear to be no clear-cut differences in the sizes and shapes of demitasse, tête-à-tête, child's tête-à-tête, and toy tea sets.

We are fortunate to be able to illustrate several (partial) R.S. Prussia toy tea sets. Some mold patterns continued to be used for a number of years, many of them beyond 1905, but rarely were they trademarked. The pattern of the set S 45, illustrated by Webb-Freyschlag, was made in two sizes. Based on the decorations of this mold, this pattern was in production from at least 1903 to 1912. Another pattern identical to an early tableware pattern, Mold OM 13, was in production from 1898 through at least 1904. The tea set we illustrate here has a decor used on tableware between 1899 and 1900. Several other tea sets in this pattern are illustrated in *French and German Dolls, Dishes, and Accessories* (Lechler, 1991). In general, her dates of production for this and other R.S. Prussia toy tea sets are at odds with our source materials[12]. Collectors having an interest in the age of their R.S. Prussia toy tea sets can find more realistic dates of manufacture in Appendix 4.

Inexpensive toy tea sets selling from 50 cents to two dollars **per dozen** sets were small, and contained from 7 to 21 pieces. Today, these sets are frequently up-graded to "doll" or "doll-size" sets[13]. As a rule, only the cup/saucer sets of the smallest toy tea sets are the same size as miniature cup/saucer sets. The miniature cup/saucer sets can be distinguished from toys by their elaborate shapes and colors, as well as a complete absence of pots, plates, and cream and sugar sets in the corresponding patterns. We know of at least four patterns used for miniatures. We suspect they were likely to have been made after 1905. We plan to show these very scarce items in a later publication.

Many new R.S. Prussia mold patterns were readied for the 1904 season. We know 16 patterns primarily by their continued use into years where examples were trademarked with the red classic RS Prussia Wreath. Of these, four molds have not been numbered[14]. We designate these molds as Mold RS 20 through Mold RS 23. As might be expected, the balance have been already been assigned RSP Mold numbers. Many of these mold patterns are illustrated in other reference books on R.S. Prussia, so we do not show many examples.

Two 1904 mold patterns, the "Lily" and "Stippled Floral," were used extensively and deserve further comment. Collectors can hardly escape including an example of the Lily mold, RSP Mold 29, in their collection. The decoration of this mold ranges from very simple floral patterns with little background color, to extraordinary examples decorated with portraits and various types of golds. We have included many of the more collectible examples of this mold in order to fully illustrate the different types of decoration Reinhold's firm was capable of producing. Oddly, very few examples of this mold may be found with an R.S. Prussia trademark. More commonly, one finds other trade names such as Royal Suhl Germany, Royal Leipsic Germany, Royal Erfurt Germany, Royal Frankfort Germany, Royal Saxe Germany, Viersa, and Royal Vienna Germany. Some of these marks include a crown in the design. However, many of the most ornate examples of this mold are not marked at all.

Prior to 1900, and a few years after, chocolate pots were sold without matching cups. Even when the sale of sets became more prevalent, the mold of the cup/saucer sets did not always match the mold of the chocolate pot. We have seen illustrations of chocolate pots in catalogs under the heading of "Coffee or Chocolate" pots. This dual use explains the appearance of chocolate pots with matching coffee cup/saucer sets, as well as coffee pots with matching chocolate cup/saucer sets. Catalog illustrations of the latter appear under the heading of "high coffees or chocolate cups". We think the coffee set shown in Plate 340 is exactly as originally sold. The matching cream/sugar set, however, was sold separately.

The Lily mold is one of the first molds to appear with the Artist Portrait transfers as part of the decoration. These transfers were most likely obtained from the firm of C.A. Pocher, located in Nürnberg, Germany. We are fortunate to be able to illustrate a page from their catalog showing the Artist Portrait transfers in Appendix 3. The small size portraits of LeBrun (2), Potocka, and Recamier were available in strips of four. These transfers had to be cut apart prior to application, and in the process, they may not have been kept in order. Consequently, where four or more small portraits were required (as in reserves), the four different portraits may not have been used. Large portraits were sold singly and in pairs. This may explain why examples of all four large portraits may not be found with one specific type of background decoration.[15]

The Stippled Floral Mold, RSP Mold 23 was used through 1906. As a result, this mold was decorated with many different decals including the Artist Portrait series used on the Lily mold. Two other innovative decorations appear on this mold. One, is the unusual cobalt and gold floral pattern shown in Plate 347. We have not recorded this pattern on any other mold. The second decoration is an outline transfer pattern of two Dutch girls shown in Plate 348. The color in this transfer, a companion to the Dutch Boy with Goose, is hand painted[16]. Objects with these two Dutch scenes are very scarce, and we suspect they were either sent here as samples, or were personally brought here from Holland[17].

There are a few instances where trade catalog illustrations are not followed by examples because we could not find them. Both mold and decorating patterns may be atypical of R.S. Prussia products, so in the absence of trademarks, collectors have not recognized them. In addition, collectors over the years may not have found examples of these few molds attractive enough to add to their collections. Items in these molds should not be thought of as rarities, however, as wholesale firms typically imported large quantities.

When making comparisons with catalog illustrations for identification, two facts must be remembered. First, pattern elements are easier to see in the catalog illustration than they are on an object, where they may be obscured by the decoration. Second, the elements of the pattern in the catalog illustration must be identical to those in the pattern of an object at hand to make a positive identification. Our experience has shown a "close" pattern match ultimately provides an incorrect identification.

Endnotes

1. The identification of items in "ES" catalog listings was made by comparison with examples known to be marked with Erdmann Schlegelmilch trademarks.

2. Descriptions in the Fall 1906 Falker and Stern Co. catalog use the term "Royal Prussian" to denote the trademark. This refers to the classic RS Prussia Wreath, rather than the RS Suhl Wreath (Capers Mark 4.1), for the latter trademark appears only on objects we know to have been produced after 1910.

3. The names for these transfers, Litta, Tillie, and Flossie, are first cited on page 212 by George Terrell Jr. in *Collecting R.S. Prussia*, (Terrell, 1982).

4. Two types of small sets were offered between 1900 and 1903. The tête-à-tête, consisting of tray, pot, cream/sugar, and two cup/saucer sets was slightly larger than the "solitaire", having only one cup/saucer set.

5. Small plates must accompany toy tea sets, otherwise they cannot be distinguished from partial tête-à-tête sets. We know of no complete toy tea sets in the Morning Glory pattern.

6. The two molds under discussion are illustrated by Mary F. Gaston's *Collectors Encyclopedia of R.S. Prussia* in Series 1 (Pt 93) and 4 (Pt 107).

7. This set is titled "Cook and Peary at North Pole" on p. 64 of *French and German Dolls, Dishes and Accessories*, (Lechler, 1991).

8. One unusual trade name is "Royal Coburg Ware Germany", (Capers mark RS 5.3(G)1).

9. One key difference between the Modified Iris and Mold RS 10 is the type of the flowers in the mold. The flower petals in Mold RS 10 protrude from the rim, and they do not in the Modified Iris pattern.

10. The Royal Berlin mark is shown on p. 179 in Series 4 of *Collector's Encyclopedia of R.S. Prussia*, (Gaston, 1995).

11. Toy tea sets offered in 1903 by Webb-Freychlag ranged from a very simple 7 piece set ($0.39 per dozen sets) to a large 23 piece combination tea and dinner set ($1.90 per set) large enough for adult use. Catalog illustrations of sets thought to be made by Reinhold's firm are provided in Appendix 4.

12. The dates of manufacture for the R.S. Prussia toy tea sets illustrated in *French and German Dolls*, range from 1898 to 1911.

13. The term "toy tea set" was used in the wholesale trade for all toy sets, regardless of size or number of pieces in a set. We can find no reference to "doll" size dishes in pre-1915 trade catalogs.

14. The balance are described by mold numbers from Series 3, *Collector's Encyclopedia of R.S. Prussia*, (Gaston, 1994) since some RSP Mold numbers in Series 1 and 2 were changed in Series 3.

15. Since large decals on items with very expensive decoration were sold individually, all four portraits might not have been used.

16. The Dutch boy with goose, illustrated in Plate 248, Series 2 (Gaston, 1986), is, to the best of our knowledge, a singular example.

17. Major markets for R.S. Prussia, other than America, were Holland and England according to B. Hartwich in *The History of the Suhl Porcelain Factories, 1861-1937*

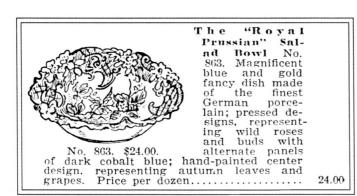

The "Royal Prussian" Salad Bowl No. 863. Magnificent blue and gold fancy dish made of the finest German porcelain; pressed designs, representing wild roses and buds with alternate panels of dark cobalt blue; hand-painted center design, representing autumn leaves and grapes. Price per dozen.................. 24.00

No. 863. $24.00.

Plate 69. Illustration of #863, cobalt blue "Royal Prussian" salad bowl in Mold RS 1 from the Spring 1900 G. Sommers & Co. catalog. *Courtesy of Minnesota Historical Society Library.*

Plate 72. Cake plate, cobalt with white center, Mold RS 2, decor HI 10, 10.25" d. RS Steeple (Prussia) in green. $250-$400.

Plate 70. Salad bowl, green/buff edge, Mold RS 1, decor P 4, 10.25" d. $150-$250.

Plate 73. Handled bowl, green underglaze, Mold RS 2, 11" d. $400-$600.

Plate 71. Salad bowl, buff/turquoise, Mold RS 1, "Spoke" decor, 10.25" d. $150-$250.

Plate 74. Cake plate, browns, Mold RS 2, decor P 1, 10.25" d. $100-$150.

Plate 75. Cake plate, green, Mold RS 2, decor P 2, 10.25" d. $100-$150.

Plate 77. Cake plate, green/purple, RSP Mold 502, no decor, 9.75" d. Marked "Royal Oldenburg" in script. $100-$150.

K2 312. Schlegelmilch's china, beautiful tulip shaped border in shaded purple and gold, green tinted base with white blossoms showing, hand-painted daisies; handles show novel perforated effect and are in ivory tint with gold tracing, set comprises ¼-pint creamer, 7½-inch covered butter and drainer, 4-inch spooner, and 5-inch sugar. 1 set in pkg.   Per set, $1.65

Plate 76. Illustration of K2 312, four piece table set in the Morning Glory mold (RSP 502, and RSP 560), from Falker and Stern Co. Fall 1903 catalog. This mold also shown in 1901-1902 G. Sommers & Co., 1903-1905 Butler Bros. catalogs. Pattern closed out by Falker and Stern Co. in 1906. *Courtesy of Amador Collections, Rio Grande Historical Collections, New Mexico State University Library.*

Plate 78. Berry set (partial), pink/buff, RSP Mold 502, spikey flower P 6 decor, master bowl 9" d., individual bowl 5" d. Full set (master plus 6 small) $250-$400.

Plate 79. Small plate, pink/yellow, RSP Mold 502, pink rose decor, 6.25" d. $50-$75.

Plate 80. Milk pitcher, pink top, RSP Mold 502, no decor, 5" h. $150-$250.

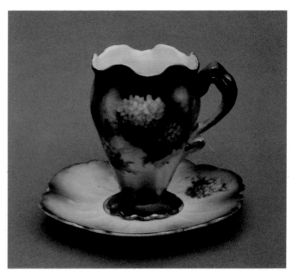

Plate 83. Chocolate cup/saucer set, green, RSP Mold 502, snowball decor, cup 3.5" h., saucer 4.5" d. $100-$150.

Plate 84. Coffee cup/saucer set, white, RSP Mold 502, wild rose decor, cup 3.5" h., saucer 5.75" d. $100-$150.

Plate 81. Chocolate pot, green/pink, RSP Mold 502, Countess Litta decor, 9.25" h. $900-$1300.

Plate 82. Chocolate pot, green/pink, RSP Mold 502, Tillie decor, 9.25" h. $900-$1300.

Plate 85. Tea cup/saucer set, green, RSP Mold 502, Countess Litta decor, cup 2.75" h. $150-$250.

Plate 88. Three handled spoon holder, light blue/buff, RSP Mold 502, small floral decor, 4.5" h. This item offered as R1031 by Butler Bros. in November 1904 catalog. $100-$150.

Plate 86. Cracker jar, green/purple, RSP Mold 502, multi-flower decor, 7.25" h. $250-$400.

Plate 87. Cracker jar, green/pink, RSP Mold 502, floral decor, 7.25" h. $250-$400.

Plate 89. Syrup pitcher set, purple/buff, RSP Mold 502, decor P 6, 5.5" h. $250-$400.

Plate 90. Mustard pot, green top, RSP Mold 502, small rose decor, 3.25" h. $100-$150.

Plate 91. Individual nut dish, green, RSP Mold 502, snowball decor, 4.75" l. Under $50.

Plate 94. Toothpick, RSP Mold 502, 2.25" h. $75-$100.

Plate 92. Match holder with striker and tray, pink edge, RSP Mold 502, small rose decor, 1.75" h., 5" l. $150-$250.

Plate 95. Salt/pepper set in greens, RSP Mold 502, 2" h. $75-$100.

Plate 93. Three handled toothpicks, RSP Mold 502, 2.25" h. $100-$150 each.

Plate 96. Three piece tea set, lavender shaded top, RSP Mold 502, pink rose decor, pot 7" h., sugar 5.25" h., cream 5.25" h. $250-$400.

Plate 97. Child's tête-à-tête (partial) set with tray, lavender shaded top, RSP Mold 502, pot 5.25" h., tray 10.25" l. Complete set $600-$900.

Below: Plate 100. Cake plate, buff/purple, RSP Mold 256, small purple flower decor, 11.5" d. $100-$150.

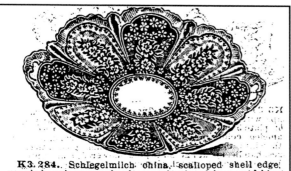

K3 284. Schlegelmilch china, scalloped shell edge, paneled surface; panels alternately tinted ivory and blue with large cluster of pink blossoms in each; gold lace border around ivory panels, center of gold lace and blue tinting with white flowers showing, gold showered edges and handles, length 11¾ inches. **Each, $1.00**

Plate 98. Illustration of K3 284 cake plate in RSP Mold 256 (also RSP Mold 451) from the Falker and Stern Co. Fall 1903 catalog. This item was closed out as Austrian trademarked china for $0.67 by Falker and Stern Co. in the Fall of 1906. Also shown in G. Sommers & Co. 1901-1905, and Butler Bros. 1903-1905 catalogs. *Courtesy of Amador Collections, Rio Grande Historical Collections, New Mexico State University Library.*

Plate 99. Cake plate, green edge, RSP Mold 256, multi-flower decor, 11.5" d. $100-$150.

Plate 101. Lidded sugar bowl, buff rim, RSP Mold 256, small red flowers, 4" h. $100-$150.

M 1318—Very fine set, consisting of 4 pieces of light weight, imported china; novel and very attractive decoration; unusually high-shaped butter dish with drainer, sugar bowl, cream pitcher and spoon holder. The cut above shows the shapes, but not the tasty decorations 1.75

Plate 102. Demitasse cup/saucer set, pink edge, RSP Mold 256, decor HI 10, cup 1.75" h, saucer 4" d. $75-$100.

Plate 105. Illustration of M 1318 four piece table set in Mold RS 6 from G. Sommers & Co. Holiday 1902 catalog. Also shown in G. Sommers 1902-1905, Butler Bros. 1903-1905, and Falker and Stern Co. 1903 catalogs. *Courtesy of Minnesota Historical Society Library.*

Plate 103. Teapot, green edge, RSP Mold 256, stylized white flowers, 4.5" h. RM. (RM.= Marked with classic R.S. Prussia Wreath) $100-$150.

Plate 104. Cracker jar, Tiffany gold edge, RSP Mold 256, small pink flower decor, 5.5" h. $600-$900.

Plate 106. Cake plate, lavender edge, Mold RS 6, two rose decor, 9.5" d. $100-$150.

Plate 107. Individual berry bowl, Mold RS 6, cupid series 2 decor, 5"
d. $75-$100.

Plate 108. Individual berry bowl, Mold RS 6, cupid series 2 decor, 5"
d. $75-$100.

Plate 109. Salad bowl, green/pink edge, Mold RS 6, drop rose decor,
10" d. $100-$150.

Plate 110. Chocolate pot, green top, Mold RS 6, two rose decor, 10"
h. $250-$400.

Plate 111. Chocolate pot, pink/buff top, Mold RS 6, drop rose decor, 10" h. $250-$400.

Plate 112. Tea pot, white, Mold RS 6, small rose decor, 7.5" h. $150-$250.

Plate 113. Three piece tea set, pink band, Mold RS 6, decor HI 13, pot 7.5" h., cream 4.5" h., sugar 5.25" h. $250-$400.

M 1546. Per Set, $2.10.

M 1546—Extra deep, 11-inch salad bowl; fine imported china; new pressed rims, edged with gold; finely decorated; six saucers to match. Price per set........................ 2.10

Plate 114. Illustration of M 1546, berry set in Mold RSP 10 from G. Sommers & Co. Fall 1902 catalog. Also shown in G. Sommers & Co. 1903-1904, and Butler Bros. 1903-1904 catalogs. Lily of the valley flowers are impressed into the mold. *Courtesy of New York State Library*.

Plate 115. Bowl, satin finish Tiffany and green, leaf shape Mold RSP 10, lily of valley decor, 9.25" w., RM. $400-$600.

Plate 118. Cracker jar, Tiffany luster edge, Mold RSP 10, white/pink rose decor, 5.75" h. $250-$400.

Plate 116. Individual berry bowl, lavenders, RSP Mold 10, small lilac decor, 5" w., RM. $50-$75.

Plate 119. Tray, lavender/yellow, Mold RSP 10, small lilac decor, 12.25" l., RM. $100-$150.

Plate 117. Sugar/cream set, satin finish Tiffany and green, Mold RSP 10, lily of valley decor, sugar 5" h., cream 4" h., RM. $400-$600.

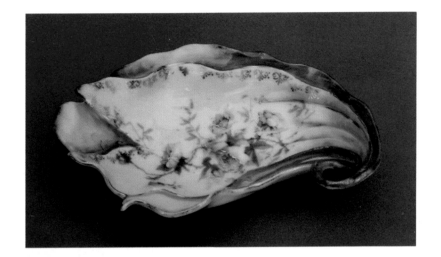

Plate 120. Individual nut tray, green edge, Mold RSP 10, small rose decor, 5.5" l. $50-$75.

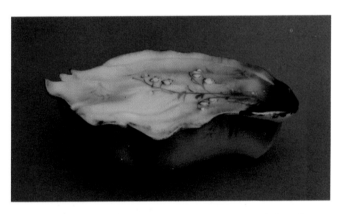

Plate 121. Box, satin finish Tiffany green, Mold RSP 10, lily of valley decor, 5.5" l. $150-$250.

K3 285. Schlegelmilch china, border of large, tinted and embossed tulips, shaded tinting with white blossoms showing and filigree gold, center ornamented with large wreath of blossoms in colors harmonizing with border, gold centerpiece, edges and handles gold showered, length 11½ inches. ¼ doz. in pkg., asst'd in lavender green and blue effects.
Each, $0.90

Plate 123. Illustration of K3 285, cake plate in Mold RS 3 from Falker and Stern Co. Fall 1903 catalog. Also illustrated in G. Sommers & Co. 1902-1904, and Butler Bros. 1903-1905 catalogs. *Courtesy of Amador Collections, Rio Grande Historical Collections, New Mexico State University Library.*

Plate 122. Chamberstick, lavender/yellow, Mold RSP 10, small lilac decor, 5" l., RM. $150-$250.

Plate 124. Plate, lavender/buff, Mold RS 3, gold medallion in center, 6.25" d. Under $50.

Plate 125. Coffee cup/saucer, Mold RS 3, small rose decor, cup 2.5" h., saucer 5.75" d. $100-$150.

M 1296. $15.00.

M 1296—Novel shaped sugar, double handled; Roman vase shape; footed, with creamer to match; sweetly decorated; finest quality imported china 15.00

FANCY 3-PIECE CHINA TEA SETS.

Plate 128. Illustration of M 1296 cream/sugar set in RSP Mold 621 from G. Sommers & Co. Fall 1902 catalog. Also shown in G. Sommers 1902-1904, and Butler Bros. 1903 catalogs. *Courtesy of Minnesota Historical Society Library.*

Plate 126. Two handled spoon holder, lavender/buff, Mold RS 3, 4.5" h. $50-$75.

Plate 129. Cracker jar, buff top, RSP Mold 621, decor P 6, 7.25" h. $250-$400.

Plate 127. Three piece tea set, turquoise/buff, Mold RS 3, pink rose decor, pot 6" h., sugar 5" h., cream 3.75" h. $400-600.

Plate 132. Chocolate pot, RSP Mold 621, small lilac decor, 9.5" h. $250-$400.

Plate 130. Cracker jar, RSP Mold 621, small lilac decor, 7.25" h. $250-$400.

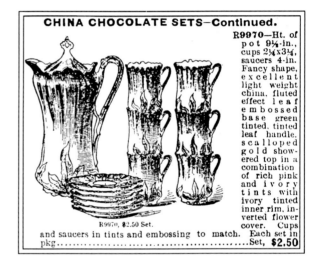

CHINA CHOCOLATE SETS—Continued.

R9970—Ht. of pot 9½-in., cups 2¼x3¼, saucers 4-in. Fancy shape, excellent light weight china, fluted effect leaf embossed base green tinted, tinted leaf handle, scalloped gold showered top in a combination of rich pink and ivory tints with ivory tinted inner rim, inverted flower cover. Cups and saucers in tints and embossing to match. Each set in pkg.........................Set, **$2.50**

R9970, $2.50 Set.

Plate 133. Illustration of R9970 chocolate set in RSP Mold 703 from Butler Bros. 1903 catalog. Also illustrated in Butler Bros. 1903-1905, G. Sommers 1902-1904, and Falker and Stern Co. 1905-1906 catalogs. *From the Collections at the Strong Museum Library.*

Plate 131. Cracker jar, RSP Mold 621, sponge finish with LeBrun portrait decor, 7.25" h. $1300-$1800.

Plate 134. Chocolate set (partial), green/buff, RSP Mold 703, rose chain decor, pot 9.75" h., cup 3.25" h., saucer 4.5" d. Complete set $200-$400.

38

Plate 135. Demitasse cup/saucer set, green, RSP Mold 703, snowball decor, cup 2.25" h, saucer 4" d. $75-$100.

K3 207. Schlegelmilch's finest, fancy green tinted border dotted with gold-centered white blossoms and edged with gold lines and fine gold lace, additional border ornamentation of large blossoms, covered with gold, center decorated with sprays of pink verbenas, edges and handle traced with gold; set comprises ⅓-pint creamer, 6-inch bowl and 7½-inch plate. **Per set, $1.40**

Plate 138. Illustration of K3 207 mush set in Mold RS 5 from the Falker and Stern Co. Fall 1903 catalog. Also illustrated in G. Sommers & Co. 1902-1904, Butler Bros. 1903-1904 catalogs. *Courtesy of Amador Collections, Rio Grande Historical Collections, New Mexico State University Library.*

Plate 136. Cracker jar, satin Tiffany finish, RSP Mold 703, lily of valley decor, 7" h. Marked Royal Vienna with crown. $900-$1300.

Plate 139. Chamberstick, magenta rim, Mold RS 5, decor P 6, 5.25" d. $250-$400.

Plate 137. Mustard pot, satin Tiffany finish, RSP Mold 703, lily of valley decor, 3.75" h. $150-$250.

Plate 140. Hair receiver, green, Mold RS 5, small rose decor, 2.25" h. $75-$100.

Plate 141. Teapot, green with pink flowers in rim, Mold RS 5, pink rose decor, 5" h. $150-$250.

Plate 142. Lemonade pitcher, blue with lavender flowers in rim, Mold RS 5, multi-flower decor, 6" h. $250-$400.

Plate 144. Cake plate, yellow/turquoise, Mold RS 7, yellow aster decor, 9.5" d. Under $50.

FINE QUALITY CAKE PLATES.

A few special numbers. Striking shape and decoration.

M 1440. $8.40 Doz.   M 1439. $12.00 Doz.

M 1440—A novel shell shape plate, measuring 11½ inches, with gold leaf handle; decoration representing large leaves in lustre, gold cat-tails and six bunches of colored flowers; crinkled edges with gold splashing; ½ dozen in package...................... 8.40

Plate 143. Illustration of M 1440 cake plate in Mold RS 7 from G. Sommers & Co. Fall 1904 catalog. Also illustrated in Sommers 1902-1905, Butler Bros. 1903-1904, and Falker and Stern Co. 1905-1906 catalogs. *Courtesy of Minnesota Historical Society Library.*

Plate 145. Cake plate, turquoise/buff, Mold RS 7, two rose decor, 11.25" d. $150-$250.

Plate 147. Bowl, green rim, Mold RS 7, small rose decor, 10.5" d. $250-$400.

M 1217. $3.00.   M 1218. $3.50.

M 1217—An assortment of very pretty, new shaped cups with fancy daisy and gold handles; pinched panels; gold lace edges; delicate tints 3.00
M 1218—A very pretty novelty cup, floral shape; beautiful new decoration; saucer to match 3.50

Below: Plate 146. Bowl, Tiffany gold rim, Mold RS 7, pink/white floral decor, 10.5" d. $400-$600.

Plate 148. Illustration of demitasse cup/saucer sets M 1217 and M 1218 from G. Sommers & Co. Fall 1902 catalog. The shape of M 1218, RSP Mold 660, is also illustrated in Butler Bros. Fall 1903 catalog and are often trademarked. *Courtesy of Minnesota Historical Society Library*.

Plate 149. Demitasse cup/saucer set, RSP Mold 660, decor P 6, 2" h., saucer 4" d. $75-$100.

Plate 150. Demitasse cup/saucer set, RSP Mold 660, decor HI 13, cup 2" h., saucer 4" d. $75-$100.

Plate 151. Demitasse cup/saucer set, RSP Mold 660, small orange flower decor, cup 2" h., saucer 4" d. $75-$100.

Plate 152. Demitasse cup/saucer set, light green background, pink blossom decor, cup 1.62" h., saucer 4" d. $75-$100.

Plate 153. Demitasse cup/saucer set, light green luster background, small rose decor, cup 2.5" h., saucer 4" d. $75-$100.

Plate 154. Demitasse cup/saucer set, turquoise/buff with gold seahorse handle, cup 2" h., saucer 4" d. $75-$100.

Plate 155. Shaving mug, green/pink background, no mold number, Flossie "Italian Head" decor, 3.5" h. $250-$400.

Plate 156. Chamberstick, light blue with purple flower, no mold number, two pink rose decor, 5.25" d. $250-$400.

Plate 158. Illustration of No. RS216 and RS217, combination candlesticks from Falker and Stern Co. Spring 1901 catalog. No complete sets are known. *Courtesy of Amador Collections, Rio Grande Historical Collections, New Mexico State University Library.*

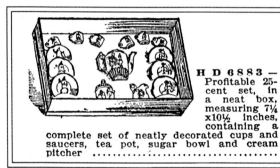

Plate 159. Illustration of HD 6883 child's toy tea set from G. Sommers & Co. Fall 1902 catalog. *Courtesy of Minnesota Historical Society Library.*

Plate 157. Chamberstick, white/fuchsia edge, no mold number, pink rose decor, 2.5" h, 4.75" l. $150-$250.

Plate 160. Child's toy tea set with post-1905 fruit decoration. Pot is 3.25" h., cream 1.62" h., cup 1" h., saucer 2.5" d., plate 3.5" d. Complete set 11 pc. (with lidded sugar) as shown in catalog illustration, with this decor $900-$1300.

Plate 161. Child's toy tea set with hand painted decoration. Pot is 3.25" h., cream 1.62" h., sugar 1.25" h. Set of 16 pc. $150-$250.

Plate 162. Partial child's toy tea set, cobalt colors, Mold OM 7, portrait of colonial lady, sugar 2.5" h., plate 2.75" d., cup 1.25" h, saucer 3" d. Complete toy tea sets with cobalt colors are very scarce.

Plate 163. Cake plate, satin finish with buff rim, RSP Mold 504, pink rose decor, 10.5" d. $250-$400.

Plate 164. Berry set (partial), RSP Mold 504, multi-flower decor, 9" d. Complete set $250-$400.

Plate 165. Candy dish, Tiffany gold rim, RSP Mold 504, pink/white rose decor, 6.25" l. $75-$100.

Plate 166. Syrup pitcher (partial set), bright pink, RSP Mold 504, 4" h. $75-$100.

Plate 167. Lemonade pitcher, light pink, RSP Mold 504, 5" h. $150-$250.

Right: Plate 168. Chocolate pot, pink top, RSP Mold 504, Easter lily decor, 9" h. $400-$600.

Below: Plate 169. Chocolate cup/saucer set, green edges, RSP Mold 504, cup 3.25" h., saucer 4.5" d. $75-$100.

Plate 170. Tea cup/saucer set, white, RSP Mold 504, pink/white rose decor, cup 3" h., saucer 6" d. $100-$150.

Plate 171. Demitasse cup/saucer set, white, RSP Mold 504, pink/white flower decor, cup 2" h., saucer 4" d. $100-$150.

Plate 174. Sugar bowl, light green, RSP Mold 504, 2.5" h. $75-$100.

Plate 175. Tray, light green, RSP Mold 504, green bow, 6" l. $100-$150.

Plate 172. Coffee cup/saucer set, green edges, RSP Mold 504, aster decor, cup 2.75" h., saucer 5.75" d. $100-$150.

Plate 173. Hair receiver, satin finish, RSP Mold 504, 5.75" l. $150-$250.

Plate 176. Gravy boat and underplate, purple, RSP Mold 504, multi-flower decor, boat 4.25", underplate 6" l. $150-$250.

Left: Plate 177. Mustard pot, pink, RSP Mold 504, pink floral decor, 3.5" h. $250-$400.

Right: Plate 180. Cracker jar, green rim, RSP Mold 571, small pink chain of roses decor, 7.25" h. $250-$400.

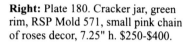

K3 220. A paneled design in Schlegelmilch china, with shell, fluted top, and side ornaments, panels tinted in shaded green with white blossoms showing, neck in pink, base in ivory, cover in green with pink knob, carnations in rich coloring. gold lace border around edge of panels, gold darts, gold tracing and gold showered edges and knobs. Dimensions 6x7.

Each, $1.05

Plate 178. Illustration of K3 220 cracker jar in RSP Mold 571 from Falker and Stern Co. Fall 1903 catalog. Also illustrated in Butler Bros. 1903-1904 catalogs. *Courtesy of Amador Collections, Rio Grande Historical Collections, New Mexico State University Library.*

Plate 181. Teapot, green/buff rim, RSP Mold 571, small pink chain of roses decor, 6.5" h. $250-$400.

Plate 179. Berry set (partial), green/buff edge, RSP Mold 571, two pink rose decor, master 10" d., individuals 5" d. $250-$400.

Plate 182. Tea cup/saucer set, buff top, RSP Mold 571, lady with orange Poppy flowers in hair, cup 2.5" h., saucer 6" d. $150-$250.

Plate 183. Tea cup/saucer set, buff top, RSP Mold 571, lady with comb in hair, cup 2.5" h., saucer 6" d. $150-$250.

Plate 184. Tea cup/saucer set, lavender/buff top, RSP Mold 571, small rose decor, cup 2.25" h., saucer 5.37" d. $100-$150.

Plate 186. Chocolate pot, Mold RS 8, two pink rose decor, 9.75" h. $250-$400.

K3 71. Schlegelmilch china, showing new "insertion" effect embossed border, ivory tinted ground clouded in richer colors behind large pink floral transfers, insertion figures tinted in light green and lavishly gold traced, surface dotted with gold stars, size 10⅜-inches. ¼ doz. in pkg., asst'd in blue, green and pink clouding.
Each, $1.00

Plate 187. Illustration of K3 71, salad bowl in RS Steeple Mold 5 from Falker and Stern Co. Fall 1903 catalog. Also shown in Butler Bros. November 1903 catalog. *Courtesy of Amador Collections, Rio Grande Historical Collections, New Mexico State University Library.*

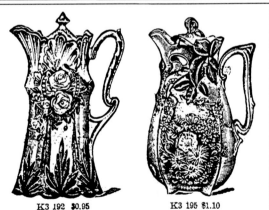

K3 192 $0.95   K3 195 $1.10
K3 192. Schlegelmilch china, new tall leaf embossed design, with wreath of embossed green leaves around base, large centerpiece of roses on shaded background, handle, knob, edge of cover and top showered with gold, capacity 2 pints. **Each, $0.95**
K3 195. Schlegelmilch beauty and originality, fancy open-work border and handle with berry and leaf and scroll embossed figures, capacity over 2½ pints, decoration—border in pink and ivory with embossed green leaves, green tinted handle, large cluster of dahlias in rich enameled colors on shaded blue background, small purple trailing flowers, edges, handle and embossing traced with gold. **Each, $1.10**

Plate 185. Illustration of K3 192, chocolate pot in Mold RS 8 from Falker and Stern Co. Fall 1903 catalog. Also shown is K3 195, chocolate pot in RSP Mold 347 (or Mold 675). This mold also in Butler Bros. 1903, and G. Sommers & Co. Fall 1904 catalogs. *Courtesy of Amador Collections, Rio Grande Historical Collections, New Mexico State University Library.*

Plate 188. Salad bowl, cobalt, RS Steeple Mold 5, water lily decor, 10.5" d. $400-$600.

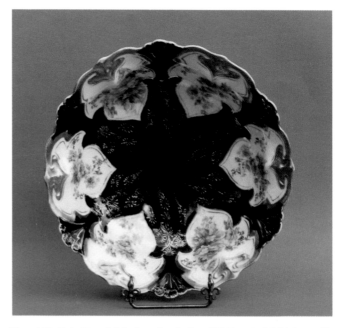

Plate 190. Salad bowl, black spoke design, RS Steeple Mold 5, small orange roses, 10.5" d. $150-$250.

Plate 191. Oval bun tray, cobalt, RS Steeple Mold 5, pink/yellow floral spray, 12.5" l. $400-$600.

Plate 189. Salad bowl, gold rim, RS Steeple Mold 5, pink rose decor, 9.75" d. $150-$150.

Plate 192. Illustration of 924 "Art Design" salad bowl in RS Steeple Mold 2 from Webb-Freyschlag Fall 1903 catalog. Also illustrated in Butler Bros. Nov. 1903, and Falker and Stern Co. Fall 1903 catalogs. *Courtesy of Amador Collections, Rio Grande Historical Collections, New Mexico State University Library.*

924. Art Design. Fancy shaped, with flaring sides, high embossed water flowers, leaves and vines in rich colors and gold on flange, heavy gold traced scalloped edge, finished in the new peacock blue and green iridescent mottled tints, center decorated with full length hand-painted portraits, finished in handsome colors, inclosed in solid gold floral wreath, extra fine grade transparent china, size 10⅜ inches in diameter; a work of art in china; price each.. 2.00

924, $2.00 each.

49

Plate 193. Salad bowl, buff rim, RS Steeple Mold 2, small pink roses decor, 10.5" d. Marked RS Steeple Germany (red). $150-$250.

Plate 195. Salad bowl, black, RS Steeple Mold 2, orange roses decor, 10.5" d. $150-$250.

Plate 196. Illustration of R168 "Orchids" cake plate in RS Steeple Mold 10 (also RS Steeple Mold 15) from Butler Bros. Nov. 1903 catalog. Also shown in Webb-Freyschlag Fall 1903, and Falker and Stern Co. Fall 1903 catalogs. *Courtesy of New York State Library.*

Plate 197. Cracker jar, gold rim, RS Steeple Mold 10, pink rose decor, 7.25" h. $250-$400.

Plate 194. Salad bowl, Tiffany bronze finish, RS Steeple Mold 2, Lady Watering Flowers decor, 10.5" d. $900-$1300.

Plate 201. Illustration of R9620 three piece tea set in RSP Mold 505 from Butler Bros. Fall 1903 catalog. Also illustrated in G. Sommers & Co. Fall 1904 catalog. *Courtesy of New York State Library.*

Plate 198. Plate, cobalt, RS Steeple Mold 10, pink/yellow floral decor, 8.5" d. $250-$400.

Plate 199. Tea cup/saucer set, lavender/buff colors, RS Steeple Mold 10, pansy decor, cup 2.12" h., saucer 6.25" d. $100-$150.

Plate 202. Sugar bowl, purple/white top, RSP Mold 505, pink/white rose decor, 4.5" h. Marked "Royal Vienna" with crown. $50-$75.

Plate 200. Three piece tea set, gold edges, RS Steeple Mold 10, small pink rose decor, pot 6" h., sugar 4.5" h., creamer 3.75" h. $400-$600.

Plate 203. Cream pitcher, RSP Mold 505, Colonial games decor, 4.5" h. $75-$100.

Plate 205. Square cake plate, gold rim, RS Steeple Mold 7, orange poppy decor, 10.25" d. Marked RS Steeple Germany (red). $150-$250.

Plate 204. Cake plate, red/buff rim, RS Steeple Mold 7 (RSP Mold 520), 10.5" d. Marked RS Steeple Germany (red). $250-$400.

Plate 206. Square cake plate, cobalt, RS Steeple Mold 7, pink/yellow floral decor, 10.25" d. $400-$600.

Plate 207. Mush (or bread and milk set), purple luster edges, RS Steeple Mold 7, multi-floral decor, pitcher 3.37" h., bowl 4.75 h., plate 6.75" d. $250-$400.

Plate 208. Tankard, cobalt, RS Steeple Mold 7, pink/yellow floral decor, 11.25" h. $2500+

Plate 209. Demitasse cup/saucer set, buff/red, RS Steeple Mold 7, tulip decor, cup 2.12" h., saucer 4.25" d. Marked RS Steeple Germany (red). $100-$150.

Plate 210. Mustard pot, red edge, RS Steeple Mold 7, orange rose decor, 3.37" h. Marked RS Steeple Germany (red). $150-$250.

Plate 211. Handled tray, cobalt rim, RS Steeple Mold 7, pink flower decor, 6.5" d. Marked RS Steeple Germany (red). $150-$250.

Plate 212. Toothpick, cobalt, RS Steeple Mold 7, pink/yellow floral decor, 2.25" h. Marked RS Steeple Prussia (red). $250-$400.

Plate 213. Salad bowl, turquoise/white, RS Steeple Mold 7, tulips decor, 10.5" d. $150-$250.

Plate 214. Salad bowl, sponge gold rim, RS Steeple Mold 7, orange poppy decor, 10.5" d. $150-$250.

Plate 215. Illustration of A 37, chocolate pot in RS Steeple Mold 14 from Webb-Freyschlag Fall 1903 catalog. This mold is also shown in Butler Bros. 1903-1904 catalogs. *Courtesy of Amador Collections, Rio Grande Historical Collections, New Mexico State University Library.*

Plate 216. Cake plate, blue with buff center, RS Steeple Mold 14, orange poppies decor, 11" d. $250-$400.

Plate 217. Cracker jar, brown, RS Steeple Mold 14, orange poppies decor, 7.5" h. $250-$400.

Plate 218. Toothpich holder, green/buff, RS Steeple Mold 14, pink flowers decor, 2.25" h. $100-$150.

Plate 221. Open handled bowl, green/buff, Mold RS 9, two pink rose decor, 11.5" d. $100-$150.

Plate 219. Cream/sugar set, cobalt, RS Steeple Mold 14, painted pink/yellow floral, sugar 5" h., cream 4" h. $400-$600.

Plate 220. Illustration of R3515, salad bowl in Mold RS 9 from Butler Bros. 1903 catalog. *From the Collections at the Strong Museum Library.*

Plate 222. Tea cup/saucer set, green/yellow, Mold RS 9, cup 2.5" h., saucer 5.75" d. $75-$100.

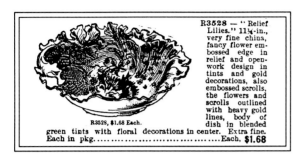

R3528 — "Relief Lilies." 11¼-in., very fine china, fancy flower embossed edge in relief and open-work design in tints and gold decorations, also embossed scrolls, the flowers and scrolls outlined with heavy gold lines, body of dish in blended green tints with floral decorations in center. Extra fine.
Each in pkg.................................Each, $1.68

R3528, $1.68 Each.

Plate 223. Illustration of R3528, salad bowl with extended petals in Mold RS 10 from Butler Bros. 1903 catalog. Not offered in 1904. *From the Collections at the Strong Museum Library.*

Plate 225. Salad bowl, turquoise rim, Mold RS 10, multi-flower decor, 11" d. $400-$600.

K3 482. Schlegelmilch's fine china, colored polkadot edge showered with gold, shaded blue-tinted border with white blossoms showing, surface dotted with pink roses, solid gilt panel, gold traced open handles. Dimensions 5¾x12¼. Each, $0.90

Plate 226. Illustration of celery tray K3 482, RS Steeple Mold 26 (RSP Mold 51 and 52) from Falker and Stern Co. Fall 1903 catalog. *Courtesy of Amador Collections, Rio Grande Historical Collections, New Mexico State University Library.*

Plate 224. Salad bowl, green/buff, Mold RS 10, yellow/white roses, 11" d. $400-$600.

Plate 227. Salad bowl, yellow with white rim, RS Steeple Mold 26, Nymph (on rock) Figural decor, 10" d. $1300-1800, rare.

Plate 228. Charger, cobalt, RS Steeple Mold 26, painted pink/yellow floral, 12" d. $600-$900.

Plate 229. Cake plate, gold rim, RS Steeple Mold 26, pink poppies, 10.5" d. $250-$400.

Plate 231. Charger, cobalt, RS Steeple Mold 26, water lily decor, 12" d. $600-$900.

Plate 232. Mug, green edge, RS Steeple Mold 26, tulips decor, 3.37" h. $75-$100.

Plate 230. Cake plate, green/red rim, RS Steeple Mold 26, tulips decor, 11.25" d. $250-$400.

Right: Plate 235. Salad bowl, cobalt, RS Steeple Mold 9, painted pink/ yellow floral, 10.5" d. Marked RS Steeple Germany (red). $400-$600.

Plate 233. Chocolate pot, turquoise/white, RS Steeple Mold 26, small pink rose decor, 9.5" h. $250-$400.

Right: Plate 236. Salad bowl, gold border, RS Steeple Mold 9, pink floral decor, 10" d. $150-$250.

913. Salad Bowl.
Artistic high embossed scrolls and water flowers finished in gold and colors on rim over tinted background; for center decoration large bouquet of hand painted tulips and roses in rich colors, extra fine grade, transparent china, size 8½ inches in diameter. Will easily bring 75 cts. ½ dozen in packages; per doz..................... 4.25

913, $4.25 per doz.

Plate 234. Illustration of 913, salad bowl in RS Steeple Mold 9 from Webb-Freyschlag Fall 1903 catalog. Also shown in Falker and Stern Co. Fall 1903 catalog. *Courtesy of Amador Collections, Rio Grande Historical Collections, New Mexico State University Library.*

Right: Plate 237. Salad bowl, rust/ white, RS Steeple Mold 9, tulips decor, 10.5" d. $100-$150.

Plate 240. Illustration of K3 60, salad bowl in Mold RS 11 from Falker and Stern Co. Fall 1903 catalog. Also shown in Butler Bros. 1903-1904 catalogs. *Courtesy of Amador Collections, Rio Grande Historical Collections, New Mexico State University Library.*

Plate 238. Salad bowl, buff/turquoise rim, RS Steeple Mold 9, poppies decor, 10.5" d. \$150-\$250.

Plate 241. Square bowl, cobalt, Mold RS 11, water lily decor, 11.5" l. \$900-\$1300.

Plate 239. Salad bowl, buff/turquoise rim, RS Steeple Mold 9 with perforated edge, pink floral decal, 10.5" d. \$250-\$400.

Plate 242. Salad bowl, cobalt, Mold RS 11 variation, painted pink/yellow floral, 10" d. \$600-\$900.

Plate 245. Salad bowl, green/white rim, Mold RS 12, orange rose decor, 10" d. Marked RS Steeple Germany (red). $150-$250.

Plate 243. Salad bowl, cobalt, Mold RS 11 variation, water lily decor, 9.5" d. Examples with perforated edges are known. $600-$900.

Plate 246. Salad bowl, green rim, Mold RS 12, pink rose decor, 10" d. $100-$150.

921. Salad Bowl. Fancy embossed scrolls tinted in yellow and outlined in gold over green tinted ground on flange, which is decorated with flowers in cameo effect, solid gold and raised enamel. heavy gold tracing on edge, large bouquet of daisies, roses, buds and leaves in beautiful colors over tinted ground for center decoration, finest grade transparent china, size 10⅜ inches in diameter, ⅙ dozen in package; per doz...........15.00

921, $15.00 doz.

Plate 244. Illustration of 921, salad bowl in Mold RS 12 from Webb-Freyschlag Fall 1903 catalog. *Courtesy of Aador Collections, Rio Grande Historical Collections, New Mexico State University Library.*

R935 — Sugar 4½-in., pitcher 3¼. 3⅜-in. opening, low shape but good capacity. Very fine transparent china, 4 green luster and gold feet, rich combination decorations of pink luster, wide band around center decorated with gold, gold band each side followed by wreath of gold stars and gold lace work. Italian head on front and back (2 subjects), medallion effect in raised gold framework, green luster and solid bands around top with fancy gold edge, tinted gold striped handles. Ultra artistic. Each set in pkg. Set, **$1.00**

R935, $1.00 Set.

Plate 247. Illustration of R935, sugar/cream set with "Flossie" Italian Head portrait in Mold RS 17 from Butler Bros. Nov. 1903 catalog. *Courtesy of New York State Library.*

Plate 248. Sugar bowl, lavender/white, Mold RS 17, "Flossie" decor, 4.25" h. $75-$100.

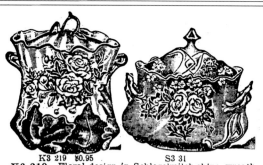

Plate 249. Illustration of K3 219, cracker jar in Mold RS 18 from Falker and Stern Co. Fall 1903 catalog. This mold illustrated in Butler Bros. 1903-1904 catalogs. Also shown is S3 31, cracker jar in Mold RS 6. *Courtesy of Amador Collections, Rio Grande Historical Collections, New Mexico State University Library.*

Right: Plate 250. Three piece tea set, lavender edge, Mold RS 18, teapot 7.25" h., sugar 5", pitcher 4.25". $250-$400.

Plate 251. Chocolate set, green ivy base, Mold RS 18, two pink rose decor, pot 10.25" h., cup 3.5" h., saucer 4.5" d. Complete set with 6 cup/saucer sets, $400-$600.

Plate 252. Cracker jar, green ivy base, Mold RS 18, small flower decor, 7" h. $400-$600.

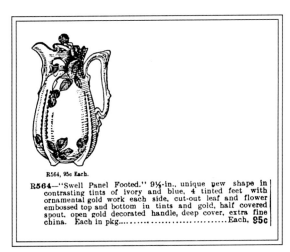

R564, 95c Each.

R564—"Swell Panel Footed." 9½-in., unique new shape in contrasting tints of ivory and blue, 4 tinted feet with ornamental gold work each side, cut-out leaf and flower embossed top and bottom in tints and gold, half covered spout, open gold decorated handle, deep cover, extra fine china. Each in pkg................................Each, 95c

Plate 255. Plate, blue/lavender, RSP Mold 347, transfer outline swans decor, 7.75" d. $150-$250.

Plate 253. Illustration of R564 chocolate pot in RSP Mold 347 (also RSP Mold 657) from Butler Bros. 1903 catalog. Also shown in Butler's 1904, Falker and Stern Co. 1903-1906, and C.E. Wheelock 1903 catalogs. *From the Collections at the Strong Museum Library.*

Plate 254. Plate, green/buff, RSP Mold 347, Easter lily decor, 9.75" d. $100-$150.

Plate 256. Salad bowl, RSP Mold 347, transfer outline swans decor, 10.75" d. (max). $400-$600.

Plate 257. Cracker jar, RSP Mold 347, transfer outline swans decor, 6.5" h. This cracker jar was carried by Butler Bros. in 1904 as R1098 priced at $1.75 each. $1300-$1800.

Plate 259. Gravy boat (partial set), RSP Mold 347, transfer outline swans decor, 6" l. Complete set with underplate $250-$400.

R9627—"Egyptian Urn Shape." Teapot 6¼-in., sugar bowl 5¼, cream pitcher 4½. Superior china, extra richly decorated in wide and narrow green bands covered with gold tracings and juvenile ornaments and followed by wreath of gold ferns, gold lacework and bands, watteau picture front in gold framework, decorated base, gold edge with ivory band, tinted and gold decorated handles and spout. Covers to match. Each set in pkg. .... Set, $2.20

Plate 260. Illustration of R9627, tea set in RSP Mold 601 with Colonial games decor from Butler Bros. Fall 1904 catalog. Also shown in Butler's 1903, and C.E. Wheelock 1903 catalogs. *Courtesy of New York State Library.*

Plate 258. Cracker jar, lavender rim, RSP Mold 347, small pink flower decor, 6.5" h. Marked classic RS Prussia Wreath. $250-$400.

Plate 261. Three piece tea set, RSP Mold 601, pink roses decor, pot 6.25" h., sugar 5.5" h., pitcher 4.5" h. $250-$400.

Plate 262. Illustration of K3 61, salad bowl in RS Steeple Mold 17 from Falker and Stern Co. Fall 1903 catalog. *Courtesy of Amador Collections, Rio Grande Historical Collections, New Mexico State University Library.*

Plate 263. Salad bowl, buff/turquoise rim, RS Steeple Mold 17, pink/white floral decor, 10.5" d. Marked RS Germany (gold). $150-$250.

Plate 265. Illustration of S3 12, salad bowl in Mold RS 13 from Falker and Stern Co. Fall 1903 catalog. *Courtesy of Amador Collections, Rio Grande Historical Collections, New Mexico State University Library.*

Plate 266. Salad bowl, white/green edge, Mold RS 13, multi-floral decor, 11" d. Marked Royal Vienna Germany in gold. $150-$250.

Plate 264. Salad bowl, lavender/buff, RS Steeple Mold 17, pansy decor, 10.5" d. $150-$250.

S3 14. Schlegelmilch china, fancy cut edge, ivory tinted ground with pink tinted shell border, large transfers of pink, yellow and white roses on mottled blue and pink grounds, gold-stippled edge, size 3½x10½.
Each, $1.00

S3 15. One of Schlegelmilch's finest, pink shaded flange, and center with white blossoms showing, wreath of filigree gold lacework, canary band, gold lines, gold edge and beautiful cluster of roses, size 2⅝x10¼.
Each, $1.00

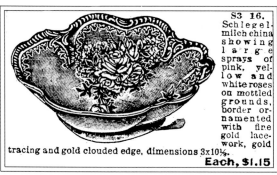

S3 16. Schlegelmilch china showing large sprays of pink, yellow and white roses on mottled grounds, border ornamented with fine gold lacework, gold tracing and gold clouded edge, dimensions 3x10½.
Each, $1.15

Plate 267. Illustration of S3 14, S3 15 and S3 16 salad bowls in Mold RS 14, RS 15, and RS 16, respectively, from Falker and Stern Co. Fall 1903 catalog. Objects in Mold RS 15 were also carried by G. Sommers & Co. in their Fall 1904 catalog. No examples of these patterns could be found for illustration. *Courtesy of Amador Collections, Rio Grande Historical Collections, New Mexico State University Library.*

MR2513. — Rich pink banded tops and bases, bodies in delicate green tint, enameled gold beading all around combined with ornamental gold wreath, ivory tinted fronts, inlaid effect with cluster of small flowers, enameled gold in lattice and scroll design, tinted inner rims, gold edges. Each set in pkg..Set, $1.89

Plate 268. Illustration of MR2513, three piece tea set in RSP Mold 616 from Butler Bros. Nov. 1903 catalog. The demitasse service in this mold is shown in Series 2, Pt. 316 of Series 2 (Gaston, 1986). *Courtesy of New York State Library.*

Plate 269. Cake plate, blue/pink, Mold RS 19, 9.75" d. $75-$100.

Plate 270. Cake plate, pink/green luster finish, Mold RS 19, 9.75" d. $100-$150.

Above left: Plate 271. Cake plate, red/yellow/green, Mold RS 19, 9.75" d. Marked Saxe Altenburg Germany (red). $75-$100.

Above: Plate 272. Heart shape salad bowl, yellow/red, Mold RS 19A, 10" d. Both flowers are poppies. $250-$400.

Above right: Plate 273. Cake plate, pink/green, Mold RS 19A, 11" d. $150-$250.

Center right: Plate 274. Cake plate, blue/yellow, Mold RS 19A, 11" d. $150-$250.

Right: Plate 275. Salad bowl, pink/buff, Mold RS 19A, 10.5" d. $250-$400.

Plate 276. Syrup pitcher (missing underplate), pink/blue, Mold RS 19A, 4.5" h. Complete set with underplate $150-$250.

Plate 279. Cup/saucer set, pink, Mold OM 151, "Tillie" Italian Head decor, 3.25" h., saucer 7" d. $150-$250.

Plate 277. Individual bowl, blue/pink, Mold RS 19A, 5.25" d. $50-$75.

Plate 280. Illustration of R868, assortment of demitasse cup/saucer sets from Butler Bros. Nov. 1903 catalog. *Courtesy of New York State Library.*

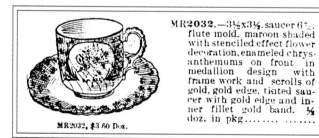

Plate 278. Illustration of MR2033 cup/saucer set in Mold OM 151 (RSP Mold 462) from Butler Bros. 1903 catalog. This pattern was made from 1898 through 1910 and carried by many wholesale firms. *From the Collections at the Strong Museum Library.*

Plate 281. Demitasse cup/saucer set, pink/white with decor P 6, cup 1.75", saucer 4" d. $50-$100.

Plate 282. Demitasse cup/saucer set, blue/white with decor P 6, cup 2.25" h, saucer 4" d. $75-$100.

Plate 283. Demitasse cup/saucer set, white, pink flowers, cup 2.25 h., saucer 4" d. $75-$100.

Plate 284. Demitasse cup/saucer set, blue/white with pink flowers, cup 1.75" h, saucer 3.75" d. $75-$100.

Plate 285. Demitasse cup/saucer set, RSP Mold 659, yellow/orange with berry decor, cup 2" h., saucer 3.5" d. $75-$100.

Right: Plate 288. Illustration of assortments of bon bon boxes from Butler Bros. Nov. 1903 catalog. One box in each assortment has an established R.S. Prussia origin. Some of these boxes were carried by Falker and Stern Co. in the same year. *Courtesy of the New York State Library.*

ST 14 $2.25

Plate 286. Illustration of ST 14, demitasse cup/saucer set from Falker and Stern Co. Fall 1903 catalog. The catalog number indicates this was unsold stock in 1903. *Courtesy of Amador Collections, Rio Grande Historical Collections, New Mexico State University Library.*

Plate 287. Demitasse cup/saucer set, pink/green, weed decor, cup 1.75" d., saucer 4" d. $75-$100.

Plate 289. Lidded box, buff, small pink rose decor, 1.5" h., 4" l. $100-$150.

Plate 292. Lidded box, pink/white roses decor, 5" l., 3.75" w. $100-$150.

Plate 290. Heart shaped lidded box, tiny roses decor, about 3.25" d. $75-$100.

Plate 293. Bon bon with handled lid, buff, RSP Mold 802 (also RSP 840), pink/white roses decor, yellow/blue flowers, 7.37" l. $150-$250.

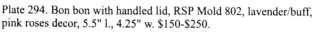

Plate 294. Bon bon with handled lid, RSP Mold 802, lavender/buff, pink roses decor, 5.5" l., 4.25" w. $150-$250.

Plate 291. Lidded box, green/pink, cherubs decor, 5.75" l., 4.25" w. $150-$250.

Plate 295. Bon bon with handled lid, RSP Mold 802, white with "Dresden" decoration inside and outside, 7.37" l. Marked with blue crown and script "D" shown in the following Plate. $250-$400.

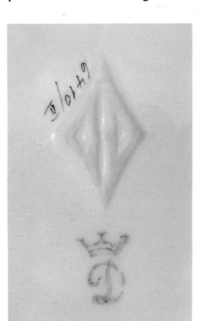

Plate 296. Blue overglaze mark on bon bon in Plate 295. One of the decorating marks of the Helena Wolfsohn firm (Dresden, Germany) who earlier specialized in producing Meissen imitations.

Plate 297. Hair receiver, turquoise/buff, RSP Mold 802, decor HI 10, 5.5" l. $100-$150.

ST 18 Bon Bon. Fine china, the shape and size of a goose egg, bottom part stands on four little feet, and cover has a handle the shape of a flower, decoration—small sprays of hand-painted flowers, handle and feet nicely gold traced, shaded tinting around center, length 4¼ inches. ½ doz. in pkg. **Per doz., $4.00**

Plate 298. Illustration of ST 18, egg shaped bon bon from Falker and Stern Co. Fall 1903 catalog. *Courtesy of Amador Collections, Rio Grande Historical Collections, New Mexico State University Library.*

BON BONS.

K3 420. ½ $2.00   K3 422. $3.50

K3 420. Bonbon. This bonbon or pin box is the product of the renowned Schlegelmilch, whose fancy china is unsurpassed. The tinted leaf and flower embossed surface, the large richly colored transfer of pansies, the gold tracing and graceful outline combine to make this one of the most successful items of our holiday line. It measures 3x5 inches and is a bargain for the money. ¼ doz. in pkg. **Per doz., $2.00**

K3 422. Bonbon. Our "50-cent" bonbon or toilet box! Size 3½x6, Schlegelmilch's fine china, fancy cut out shape, leaf and flower embossed cover, large purple flower transfers on beautiful mottled tinted grounds, lavish gold tracing. This article presents a rich and captivating appearance and will impress everyone as a quick seller. ½ doz. in pkg. asst'd tints. **Per doz., $3.50**

Plate 299. Illustration of bon bons K3 420 and K3 422 from Falker and Stern Co. Fall 1903 catalog. *Courtesy of Amador Collections, Rio Grande Historical Collections, New Mexico State University Library.*

Two Styles R225, $1.80 Doz.

R225—About 5¼-in., 6 shapes and 6 decorations Extra thin transparent china, daintiest of shapes, perforated handles, decorations in colored tints, combined with beautiful flowers, gold showered and gold scroll edges, each in effective combinations. Selected with care, sure to please. ¼ doz. in pkg, 6 styles asstd. ......Doz., **$1.80**

Two Styles R226, $2.00 Doz.

R226—About 5¼-in., 6 shapes in leaf, shell and floral designs, decorations of combination tints, colored flowers, tinted embossed flowers and gold wreaths, gold edges, fancy embossings in rich and beautiful combinations. *Exceptional value.* 6 styles asstd., ¼ doz. in pkg.......Doz., **$2.00**

Two Styles R227, $2.25 Doz.

R227—About 5¼-in., 6 shapes, various leaf and flower patterns, gold rich tinted showered handles, gold showered edges, some with tinted band borders and center decorations of tints and beautiful flowers in artistic combinations. Must be seen to be appreciated. Asstd., ¼ doz. in pkg...............Doz. **$2.25**

Plate 300. Illustration of assortments of small trays from Butler Bros. Nov. 1903 catalog. *Courtesy of New York State Library.*

Plate 301. Handled tray, RSP Mold 802, small rose decor, 6.25" l., 5" w. $75-$100.

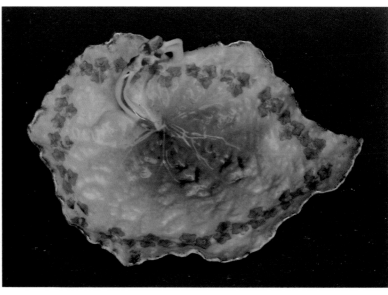

Plate 304. Tray, leaf shape, 5.5" l. Under $50.

Plate 302. Tray, white, RSP Mold 347, small rose decor, 4.62" l. Under $50.

Plate 305. Tray, green, "Litta" Italian Head decor, 6.25" l. $150-$250.

Plate 303. Tray, green edge, small roses decor, 5" l. Under $50.

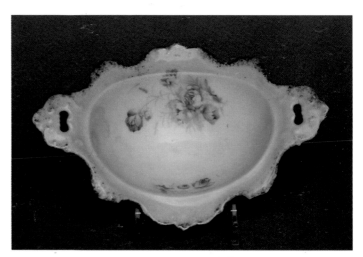

Plate 306. Tray, buff, pink/yellow rose decor, 5.5" l., 3.5" w. Under $50.

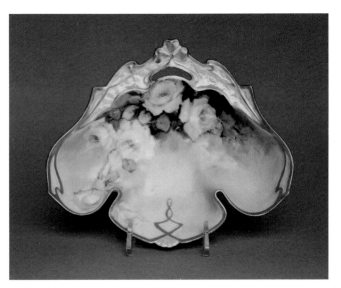

Plate 307. Tray, blue/pink, white rose painted decor, 6.25" l., 5" w. $50-$75.

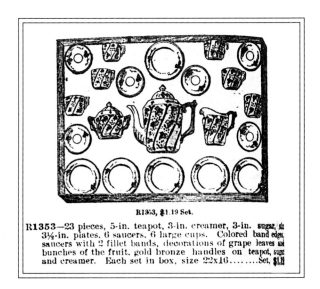

R1353, $1.19 Set.

R1353—23 pieces, 5-in. teapot, 3-in. creamer, 3-in. sugar, six 3½-in. plates, 6 saucers, 6 large cups. Colored band edges saucers with 2 fillet bands, decorations of grape leaves and bunches of the fruit, gold bronze handles on teapot, sugar and creamer. Each set in box, size 22x16........Set, $1.19

Plate 308. Illustration of R1353, Child's toy tea set from Butler Bros. Nov. 1903 catalog. This mold was used at least through 1908 as it is known with the Bluebirds decor. *Courtesy of New York State Library.*

Plate 309. China toy tea set (partial), pink roses decor, pot 5" h., sugar 3.25" h., pitcher 3" h., cup 1.75", saucer 3" d., plate 3.5" d. Complete set of 23 pcs. (without box) $600-$900.

Plate 310. China toy tea set (partial), yellow rose and bluebirds (post-1905 decor), pieces same size as in Plate 309. Complete set of 23 pcs (without box) $900-$1300.

Plate 311. China toy tea set (partial), Mold OM 7, blue/white with decor HI 13, pot 4" h. Complete set 23 pieces $600-$900.

R272—3⅝x3¼. One shape, 4 styles of decorations, contrasting colors in Venetian design with gold ornamentation and bands, wreaths and bouquets of flowers, panel and clouded effects, gold striped edges and handles. ⅙ doz. pkg. 4 00

R272, $4.00 Doz.

Plate 312. Illustration of R272, mugs with different decorations in RSP Mold 501 from Butler Bros. 1904 catalog. *Courtesy of New York State Library.*

Plate 313. Plate, blue/buff, RSP Mold 501, multi-flower decor, 7.75" d. $50-$75.

Plate 315. Cracker jar, blue/buff, RSP Mold 501, multi-flower decor, 5.5" h. $150-$250.

Plate 314. Lemonade pitcher, satin finish green/lavender, RSP Mold 501, lavender floral decor, 5" h. $150-$250.

Plate 316. Tea cup/saucer set, Tiffany band, RSP Mold 501, pink rose decor, cup 2" h., saucer 4.25" d. $100-$150.

Plate 317. Mustard pot, blue band at top, RSP Mold 501, multiflower decor, 3" h. $100-$150.

Plate 318. Illustration of R1124, sugar/cream set in RSP Mold 576 from Butler Bros. 1904 catalog. *Courtesy of New York State Library.*

R1124—Sugar 4, pitcher 3¾. Bands of green and chamois, embossed solid gold border tops, floral and gold wreaths with gold floral clusters all over, green tinted cover floral decorated, gold striped tops and open handles, fillet gold bands top and bottom. 1-6 doz. sets in pkg.

Doz. sets, **$6.75**

R1124, $6.75 Doz. Sets.

Plate 319. Cream and sugar set, blue band top and bottom, RSP Mold 576, decor HI 13, sugar 4" h., cream 3.5" h. $100-$150.

Plate 320. Teapot, RSP Mold 576, pink rose cascade decor, pot 5.37" h. $250-$400.

Plate 321. Teapot, browns, RSP Mold 576, Mill scene, pot 5.37" h. $600-$900.

74

Plate 322. Illustration of R1094, cracker jar in RSP Mold 627 from Butler Bros. Jan. 1904 catalog. Also shown in G. Sommers & Co. 1904-1905, and Webb-Freyschlag 1903 catalogs. *Courtesy of New York State Library.*

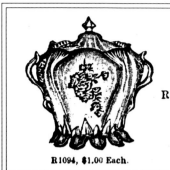

R1094, $1.00 Each.

R1094—4¾x7, footed flower shape, embossed petals, green shaded gold decorated leaf base, rose tints all over jar and cover, gold decorated inlaid panels, gold striped leaf handles, cluster of roses on jar and cover. Each in pkg..Each. **$1.00**

Plate 323. Plate, buff edge with Tiffany type flowers, RSP Mold 627, multi-flower decor, 8.25" d. $250-$400.

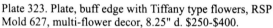

Plate 324. Cream pitcher, yellow/purple sponge effect, RSP Mold 627, Girl with Medallion in Hair portrait, 4.5" h. $100-$150.

Plate 325. Cream/sugar set, Tiffany bronze bands, RSP Mold 627, yellow/pink rose decor, cream 4.5" h., sugar 5" h. $250-$400.

Plate 326. Cracker jar, green/buff, RSP Mold 627, yellow/pink rose decor, 6.75" h. $400-$600.

Plate 327. Cracker jar, Tiffany bronze bands, RSP Mold 627, yellow/pink roses, 6.75" h. $1300-$1800.

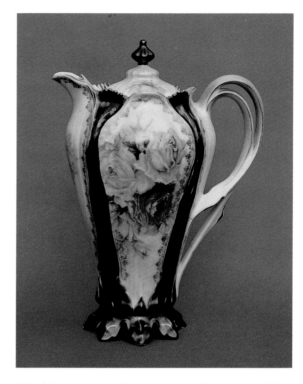

Plate 329. Chocolate pot, Tiffany bronze bands, RSP Mold 627, yellow/pink rose decor, 9" h. $600-$900.

Plate 328. Cracker jar, RSP Mold 627, red roses decor, 6.75" h. Marked classic RS Prussia Wreath. $600-$900.

Plate 330. Mustard pot, lavender/buff, RSP Mold 627, yellow rose decor, 3.25" h. $100-$150.

Another Splendid Value in
IMPORTED CHINA SALAD DISHES.
A bargain for us, for you and for your customers.

R 6 5 9 — 10½ in., paneled with embossed flowers in colors and gold, green cloud points with white foliage, large beautiful centerpiece. Extra fine and artistic. 2 in pkg.
Per dozen, **$7.60**

R682, $2.12 Each.

R682 — 10½ in., indented pattern, embossed flower columns in solid gold and colors, shaded maroon and pink points decorated with gold garlands and white flowers, picture center on solid gold band ground with gold flowers and ferns. Asstd. subjects. Each in pkg.. Each, **$2.12**

Plate 331. Illustrations of R659 (floral) and R682 (Recamier) salad bowls in RSP Mold 29 (also Mold 517) from Butler Bros. Fall 1904 catalog. *Courtesy of New York State Library.*

Plate 334. Footed salad bowl, buff/lavender, RSP Mold 29, Potocka portrait with thumbed gold background decor, 10.5" d. The identical bowl is illustrated as M 1495 in the G. Sommers & Co. Fall 1904 catalog. $900-$1300.

Plate 332. Salad bowl, Tiffany gold with blue outline flowers, RSP Mold 29, Potocka portrait decor, 11" d. $1800-$2500.

Plate 335. Salad bowl, turquoise/buff, RSP Mold 29, Flora scenic decor, 10.5" d. $1300-$1800.

Plate 333. Salad bowl, Tiffany bronze with Moire pattern overlay, RSP Mold 29, LeBrun portrait decor, 10.5" d. $1800-$2500.

Plate 336. Salad bowl, cobalt, RSP Mold 29, iris decor, 10" d. Very scarce decor in this mold. $600-$900.

Plate 338. Footed bowl, lavender with Tiffany type flowers, RSP Mold 29, Recamier portrait, 8.5" d. $900-$1300.

Plate 337. Footed bowl, Tiffany gold edge, RSP Mold 29, Lady in Red portrait decor, 7" d. Very scarce decoration $600-$900.

Plate 339. Three piece tea set, lavender with Tiffany type flowers, LeBrun (with hat) and Recamier portraits, pot 5.25" h. $1800-$2500.

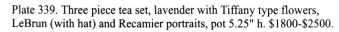

Plate 340. Coffee service with matching cream and sugar, red, RSP Mold 29, coffee 9.75"h. (LeBrun), cream 3.5" h. and sugar 5" h. (Potocka), "high coffee" cups 3" h. (LeBrun and Recamier), saucers 4.5" d. $9,000.

Right: Plate 343. Salad bowl, cobalt edge, Mold RS 20, yellow rose decor, 10.75" d. $250-$400.

R658 — 10¾ in., heavy embossed white border edge gold decorated surface in delicate combination tints with large floral centerpiece. Very fine. 1 doz. in pkg.

Doz., **$7.50**

R658, $7.50 Doz.

Plate 341. Illustration of R658, salad bowl in Mold RS 20 from Butler Bros. Fall 1904 catalog. *Courtesy of New York State Library.*

Plate 342. Salad bowl, Tiffany gold edge, Mold RS 20, pink floral decor, 10.75" d. $250-$400.

Plate 344. Salad bowl, lavender/buff, no mold number, pink floral decor, 10.5" d. $150-$250.

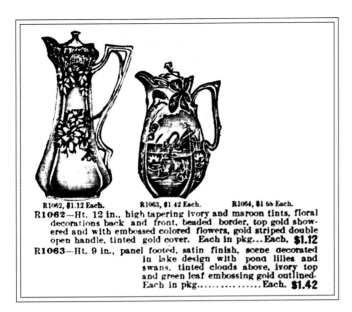

R1062, $1.12 Each.   R1063, $1.42 Each.   R1064, $1 65 Each.

R1062—Ht. 12 in., high tapering ivory and maroon tints, floral decorations back and front, beaded border, top gold showered and with embossed colored flowers, gold striped double open handle, tinted gold cover. Each in pkg...Each. **$1.12**

R1063—Ht. 9 in., panel footed, satin finish, scene decorated in lake design with pond lilies and swans, tinted clouds above, ivory top and green leaf embossing gold outlined. Each in pkg................Each. **$1.42**

Plate 345. Illustration of R1062, concave shape chocolate pot in RSP Mold 23 from Butler Bros. Fall 1904 catalog. Also shown in G. Sommers & Co. 1904-1905, and Falker and Stern Co. 1906 catalogs. Illustration includes R1063, chocolate pot in RSP Mold 657 with outline transfer of stylized swans, dating the use of this decoration. *Courtesy of New York State Library.*

Plate 347. Cake plate, cobalt flowers with gold rim, RSP Mold 23, 8.5" d. $250-$400.

Plate 346. Cake plate, cobalt with gold rim, RSP Mold 23, stylize flower decor, 11" d. $400-$600.

Plate 348. Salad bowl, red with gold rim, RSP Mold 23, outline transfer of Dutch children, 9" d. Very rare decoration. $400-$600.

Plate 349. Chocolate cup/saucer, lavender rims, RSP Mold 23, red rose decor, cup 3.5" h., saucer 4.37" d. Marked classic RS Prussia Wreath. $100-$150.

Plate 350. Chocolate pot (concave), red with gold trim, RSP Mold 23, yellow rose decor, 11.5" h. $400-$600.

Plate 353. Plate, red, RSP Mold 98, Recamier portrait, 7" d. Marked RS Steeple Germany (red) $600-$900.

Plate 351. Tray, cobalt with gold rim, RSP Mold 23, stylized flower decor, 11.5" l., 7" w. $600-$900.

Plate 354. Cake plate, gold/buff edge, RSP Mold 98, Recamier portrait, 10.75" d. Marked RS Steeple (red). $1300-$1800.

Plate 352. Illustration of R708, oval bowl with "Castle" scene in RSP Mold 98 from Butler Bros. Fall 1904 catalog. *Courtesy of New York State Library.*

Plate 355. Plate, gold/buff edge, RSP Mold 98, pink flower decor, 8" d. $250-$400.

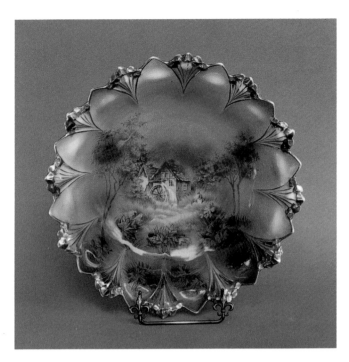

Plate 358. Salad bowl, sunset colors, RSP Mold 98, Mill scene decor, 10.25" d. $600-$900.

Plate 356. Syrup pitcher, blue edges, RSP Mold 98, pink floral decor, 5" h. $250-$400.

Plate 359. Tray, cobalt, RSP Mold 98, LeBrun portrait on gold background, 11.25" l., 7.5" w. $2500+

Plate 357. Cream/sugar set, red/gold edges, RSP Mold 98, pink rose decor, sugar 3.25" h., cream 2.25" h. $250-$400.

R670 – 11⅝ in., rural landscape picture center, asstd. subjects, chamios tinted body, ivory band border, gold edge, heavy leaf embossed pattern, gold scroll and gold cloud decorated. Each in pkg.

Each. **92c**

R670. 92c Each.

Plate 360. Illustration of R670, salad bowl with "Mill" scene in RS Steeple Mold 1 from Butler Bros. Fall 1904 catalog. *Courtesy of New York State Library.*

Plate 361. Salad bowl, buff edge, RS Steeple Mold 1, yellow rose decor, 10.5" d. $150-$250.

Plate 362. Cake plate, gold edge, RSP Mold 339, yellow rose decor, 10.5" d. $250-$400.

Plate 363. Charger, red with gold edge, RSP Mold 339, yellow rose decor, 12.25" d. $400-$600.

R1157 -- Teapot 6½, sugar 5¼, creamer 4¼. Gold banded top and foot, 2 gold lace wreaths around center, floral decoration back and front, fillet gold band at foot, decorated covers, gold striped open handles. Each set in pkg........Set, **$1.29**

R1157, $1 29 Set.

Plate 364. Illustration of R1157, three piece tea set in Mold RS 21 from Butler Bros. Fall 1904 catalog. *Courtesy of New York State Library.*

83

Plate 365. Cream pitcher, Mold RS 21, roses decor, creamer 4.25" h. $50-$75.

Plate 368. Salad bowl, purple/blue/yellow, Mold RS 23, clematis decor, 10.5" d. $150-$250.

R664 — 10½ in., crimped flower pattern, turned up rim, gold edge, old green luster body with dark green clouds, white flower decoration, embossed cosmos with yellow and gold edges, large rose centerpiece. 1-6 doz. in pkg.....Doz.. **$8.35**

R664, $8.35 Doz.

Plate 366. Illustration of R664, salad bowl in Mold RS 23 from Butler Bros. Fall 1904 catalog. Also shown in Falker and Stern Co. Fall 1906 catalog. *Courtesy of New York State Library.*

Plate 369. Illustration of R678, salad bowl with Recamier portrait in Mold RS 22 from Butler Bros. Fall 1904 catalog.

Descriptions reads: 11 1/2 in. open water lily shape, blended yellow and ivory tints, each petal with gold and red decorations, bust center on dark green background, surrounded by embossed gold outlined ornaments. Asstd. subjects. Each in package... Each $1.58. *Courtesy of New York State Library.*

Plate 370. Salad bowl, blue/buff edge, Mold RS 22, Flora and Diana in reserves, yellow rose decor, 10.5" d. $900-$1300.

Plate 367. Salad bowl, yellow/gold, Mold RS 23, yellow roses decor, 10.5" d. $250-$400.

Plate 371. Salad bowl, pink/buff, Mold RS 22, LeBrun portrait, 10.5" d. $1300-$1800.

Plate 374. Salad bowl, green/buff, RSP Mold 19, red rose decor, 11" d. $250-$400.

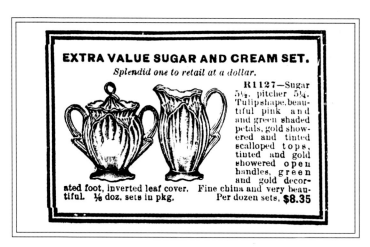

Plate 375. Illustration of R1127, sugar/cream set in "Tulip" RSP Mold 652 from Butler Bros. Jan. 1904 catalog. Also shown in Butler's 1905 catalog. *Courtesy of New York State Library.*

Plate 372. Salad bowl, pink/buff, Mold RS 22, Potocka portrait, 10.5" d. $1300-$1800.

Plate 373. Illustration of R672, salad bowl in "Sea Creature" RSP Mold 19 from Butler Bros. Fall 1904 catalog. Also shown in Butler's 1905 catalog. *Courtesy of New York State Library.*

R1314—9¼ in. pot, shaded green tints with gold scrolls on embossed pattern, colored floral decorations back and front with gold stamens, gold scroll decorated base, top, over and handle, half covered spout, footed, cups and saucers decorated all over to match. Each set in pkg.........Set, **$2.87**

R1314, $2.87 Set.

Plate 379. Illustration of R1314, chocolate set in RSP Mold 647 from Butler Bros. Fall 1904 catalog. Also shown in Falker and Stern Co. 1906 catalog. Objects in this mold with the decor shown are known to be marked with "Royal Vienna" and crown in gold. *Courtesy of New York State Library.*

Plate 376. Chocolate pot, Tiffany bronze top/bottom, RSP Mold 652, pink rose decor, 10" h. $900-$1300.

R1134 — Sugar pitcher 3¼. T green body with dallion front bossed gold deco tops with maroo lay and floral rations, solid open handles, and maroon t bases with fl wreath. Cove

R1134, $1.65 Set.

match. Each set in pkg............................Set,

Plate 377. Illustration of R1134, sugar/cream set in RSP Mold 614 with LeBrun portraits from Butler Bros. Fall 1904 catalog. Sets with flower embossed gold panels and decorations back and front were listed as R1125, and sold for $7.80 for a dozen sets. *Courtesy of New York State Library.*

Plate 378. Sugar/cream set, RSP Mold 614, small rose decor, sugar 5" h., cream 3.5" h. $150-$250.

Plate 380. Cup/saucer set, pink edges, RSP Mold 647, tiny pink flower decor, cup 1.75" h., saucer 4.25" d. $100-$150.

Plate 381. Cracker jar, blue/buff, RSP Mold 647, Easter lily decor, 6.5" h. Marked Royal Vienna with crown. $250-$400.

Chapter Three
Hidden Image and Related Mold Patterns

One of the most interesting of all R.S. Prussia Art Nouveau patterns used for tableware was sold in the United States from 1901 through 1906. Each piece incorporated an embossed cameo in the mold, usually a woman's head, surrounded by raised flowers and leaves. On many objects, the cameo is decorated so skillfully the image blends in with the rest of the decoration. Sometimes the cameo was painted over, essentially ignoring the image. For good reason, collectors use Hidden Image as a nickname for this pattern.

Hidden image is distinguished from other types of porcelain having an image in the mold by the use of a distinct set of printed floral transfers. As far as we can determine, these transfers were never used by another porcelain manufacturing firm. We do not include early examples of Reinhold's porcelain with houses in the mold. The two types of hidden house molds always seem to be decorated with outline transfers. We suspect they were precursors to the Hidden Image pattern.

In parallel to the products shown in Chapter 2, a number of product lines were manufactured from 1901 through 1904 with the same decorating patterns used for Hidden Image. For this reason, they are grouped as a subset of Hidden Image products. These related patterns were used for trademarked as well as trade named products. The appearance of a city name in the trade name, eg. Altenburg in "Saxe Altenburg Germany," has led some collectors to assume the item was made and/or decorated in the corresponding city. To date, we have been unable to find any evidence to support assumptions of this type. On the other hand, we will show how these trade names allowed Reinhold's firm to sell the same product to different American distributors.

There are some isolated examples of Hidden Image transfers on trademarked, post-1905 R.S. Prussia patterns. These few examples are important to our understanding of the merchandising of R.S. Prussia, and are grouped at the end of the chapter.

For many years, collectors were not sure Hidden Image tableware should be included with R.S. Prussia. Fraudulent marks were deemed to have been used on examples marked with the classic R.S. Prussia wreath. Examples marked with trade names could not be directly linked to Reinhold's firm. In addition, some collectors could have been misled by the abundance of poorly decorated examples, and the use of second quality china.[1] Admittedly, these attributes are atypical of R.S. Prussia. But the Hidden Image pattern was one of the most extensive lines ever produced, and we suspect it met with such demand that product quality was temporarily compromised.

Our first clue this pattern should be included with R.S. Prussia came from a systematic examination of the decoration. A report of this study was made at the 1991 Convention of the International Association of R.S. Prussia Collectors. At the time, we noted only R.S. trademarks to be associated with any of the decals, gold stencils, or painted designs used on the Hidden Image pattern. This situation has not changed in the intervening years. Any doubt of the origin was dispelled by information in the 1903 Falker and Stern Co. catalogs. In the Spring issue, the firm presents "A few words from their fancy goods buyer as to what we will show you in our Fall catalog of imported fancy goods." Under this heading, they note how they will "show you a large variety of the productions of Germany's most renowned factories. Foremost among these will be the matchless goods made by Reinhold Schlegelmilch in Suhl and Tillowitz, Germany."[2] In the Fall 1903 issue, a variety of objects in the Hidden Image pattern were offered, and all are described as Schlegelmilch china.[3]

For the most part, the production of the Hidden Image pattern was too early for objects to be trademarked with the classic RS Prussia Wreath. Although this pattern was contemporary to others marked with the RS Steeple Germany (red) trademark, we have not found any Hidden Image objects with this mark. With a single exception, the series of printed transfers used for Hidden Image ware was completely different from the series of transfers used for RS Steeple Germany molds. We think this situation reflects a restriction in the decoration of merchandise shipped under a given trademark or trade name. The only factory applied marks we know to have been used on Hidden Image ware are Saxe Altenburg and Royal Hamburg, with "Germany" denoting the country of origin[4].

It is interesting to note in the Fall of 1906, that Falker and Stern Co. close out (at reduced prices) several items in the Hidden Image pattern as "trademarked Bavarian china." If we assume the items involved were actually marked, then we must conclude Falker and Stern Co. distributed one of the two trade names indicated above[5].

Collectors today will find it difficult to locate objects in the Hidden Image pattern. Obviously, this cannot be the result of a short production run or a lack of a widespread distribution. The shortage is due primarily to the infrequent turnover of objects in the antique marketplace. In this respect, items in this pattern are similar to children's toy tea sets. Interesting items frequently become heirlooms, and remain within families for long periods of time.

Over the years of collecting information on Hidden Image ware, we were continually surprised at the year to year increase in the number of different objects that were made. Our current list of more than 50 items, reproduced in Appendix 5, is the largest of all R.S. Prussia patterns. Some of the large Hidden Image objects appear to be very scarce, owing most likely to their use in various types of eating establishments. For various reasons, we have been unable to document some of the objects. Several are based on the recollection of individuals, so these may not be accurately cataloged.

We begin Chapter 3 by illustrating a series of large, double image cake plates, each with a different decoration. Our purpose is to show the variety available, as well as the effect decoration has on the overall appearance[6]. These plates were sold as "deep cake plates", even though they look like shallow bowls. Smaller plates and cake plates follow. In keeping with other R.S. Prussia patterns, small plates, ranging from 5" to 9", are very scarce. In this size range, the competition from other china producing firms was intense, for we have seen few R.S. Prussia plates in dozens of catalog illustrations.

Most salad bowls have a single image in the rim. Berry sets are formed from the salad bowl and matching 5" individual bowls. Lidded items are difficult to find with intact finials. Examples of the sugar bowl and mustard pot shown here have damaged lids. Catalog illustrations clearly show three leaf sections in the finials of all lidded items. The difficulty in holding a lid by this type of finial partially explains why we frequently see items with damaged, repaired, or missing tops.

More sizes of pitchers are known for Hidden Image than any other R.S. Prussia pattern. We have seen, but could not locate for illustration, the bulbous pitcher sold with the bread and milk set. The lemonade pitcher holds nearly five pints, and is the largest of all regulation shaped R.S. Prussia pitchers. In spite of the large size, these pitchers are not scarce.

Cup and saucer sets are, on the other hand, very scarce. We have recorded very few examples of the demitasse and tea sizes. Chocolate cup/saucer sets are more prevalent, but it is exceptionally difficult to find a set of six to match the decoration of a chocolate pot[7]. Mugs of several kinds are often seen at specialized auctions. Hidden Image is one of the few R.S. Prussia patterns to include a half-size, mustache mug. Unlike mugs in other patterns, Hidden Image mugs seem to have been sold without matching saucers.

Trays in many sizes were made in the Hidden Image pattern. Some molds are so complex, with looping sections of stems and extended leaves, it is a wonder any examples survive intact. Beware, as damage to these items is difficult to detect. When no catalog illustration was available, we acquired several examples of each to be assured of showing the original shape.

All known sizes of boxes complete this segment of Hidden Image ware. Like trays, every size box has a different image. The heart-shaped hair receiver is one of the easiest to obtain, and may be found in a wide range of decorations. The dresser tray is not large enough to accommodate two pieces the size of the hair receiver. Consequently, we do not think the heart-shape box was made as part of a set. Other boxes are rarely decorated differently from the illustration(s) shown here.

Although cream and sugar sets were sold by G. Sommers & Co., we can find no evidence for the manufacture of either four or five piece table sets. This accounts for our inability to show a covered butter or an upright spoon holder. This is unusual, for other contemporary R.S. Prussia patterns include table sets. In the same vein, coffee and demitasse cup/saucer sets are known, but we have no record of the corresponding coffee or demitasse pots. Whether or not these sets were made is not known at this time.

Mold patterns related to Hidden Image by the use of the same set of decorating transfers form an interesting group. The known dates of sale for marked mold patterns allow us to continue to track the transition in marks used for R.S. Prussia. Beginning in 1900 and extending into 1901, a few molds trademarked (under glaze) with RS Steeple Prussia or RS Steeple Germany appear in trade catalogs. Some patterns with these trademarks have already been shown in Chapter 1. Between 1901 and 1903, cobalt decorated objects with the underglaze RS Steeple trademarks seem to have been phased out, and in their place are brightly colored decal decorated objects marked partly with the red R.S. Steeple Germany trademark, and partly with trade names. All of these marks are applied over the glaze. Only a few of all the molds known to be marked with the red RS Steeple Germany trademark appear here in Chapter 3. In principle, the red RS Steeple Germany mark could have been used beyond 1906[8]. However, this appears not to have been the case, for by this time, wholesale firms had discontinued the import of mold patterns with this mark.

In addition to manufacturing and trademark changes, the objects in these related molds show an important shift in the distribution of merchandise to American customers. Between 1900 and the end of 1902, fine china entries in the catalogs of wholesale firms increased by more than 50 percent. In the Spring of 1903, Falker and Stern Co. note "Our immense success in this line last fall almost cleaned out all old stock." The combined sales of wholesale firms must have had a very negative impact on the sales of established factory representatives (called "Drummers" or "Roadmen" at the time). In 1903, Butler Bros. prefaces the fine china section of their Fall catalog with comments indicative of the severity of the problem: "The drummer for the toy or china house, in order to explain his higher prices, may tell you our china is poorer grade. The fact is that the goods are IDENTICAL makes, same blanks, same decorations, same packages."

Seeing their sales decline, it is not difficult to imagine the factory representatives used every opportunity to talk down the merchandise from their new competitors. Quite possibly, both types of distributors were not above a little exaggeration. Many objects with very expensive types of decoration can be found in collections today, yet they do not appear in any of the trade catalogs we have examined. We suspect this china was distributed primarily by factory representatives.

Where the quality of china shipped to both types of distributors was comparable, the application of a trade name was a way for Reinhold's firm to create a point of difference. Each distributor receiving china marked with a trade name could have, from a technical point of view, merchandise not available to a competitor. We are certain the trade names shown in this book originated at Reinhold's factory, for there are occasions where a trade name and an RS trademark are found on identical items.

We now realize the trade name concept was used by Reinhold's firm to minimize the problems caused by their increased distribution of goods through wholesale firms. For many years, trade names were a source of confusion for collectors, for they appeared on mold patterns generally recognized as part of R.S. Prussia. Yet, the trade name inferred a manufacture and/or decoration at another location. This is particularly true for items marked with "Saxe Altenburg Germany." Unfortunately, this state of affairs is reflected, rather than clarified, in the most recent book by Mary F. Gaston.[9] By grouping objects according to mold pattern, rather than by mark, one can easily show how just a few tableware patterns from this period of time were marketed under a variety of trade names. In retrospect, the trade name concept must not have been too successful, for the vast majority of products made in this period are not marked in any way, and all trade names disappeared by 1905 (with the possible exception of Royal Vienna Germany).

In principle, trade name merchandise could have been sent to either factory representatives or wholesale firms. However, there are several reasons why trade name goods may have been distributed by wholesale accounts. First, the account had to be large enough to warrant the extra cost of applying the mark at the factory, as well as keeping the finished merchandise separate. Second, trade name goods may be currently found all across the United States, indicating a large area of distribution. Third, in 1906, Falker and Stern Co. closed out objects in several patterns described as trademarked "Austrian" or "Bavarian" china, in addition to the Hidden Image pattern. The Saxe Altenburg Germany trade name is common to nearly all of these items[10]. If these goods were actually marked[11], then Falker and Stern Co. must have been one of the firms carrying Saxe Altenburg Germany marked merchandise.

Overall, we know of about a dozen trade names to be used on about an equal number of mold patterns[12]. A very large percentage of these patterns appear in this chapter. Many of these marks are reproduced in Appendix 6. Most applied marks were printed in red (red-orange) enamel. We are quite sure the marks were applied at the factory. Merchandise orders placed with factory representatives were shipped directly to the retail account, as there was no distribution center in the United States at this time. In addition, there is ample evidence from ordering instructions in wholesale catalogs to indicate packages shipped directly from the manufacturer were not repackaged for shipment to retailers.

One might wonder how Reinhold's firm could control the merchandise sent to various distributors under different trade names. This key problem was obviated by the sample program used by European manufacturers to sell into the American market. We have noted earlier the shipment of sample goods to wholesale firms at the beginning of each calendar year[13]. These samples were made from production, or pre-production, full size molds[14]. The simple restriction of samples would allow each manufacturing firm to control all of the merchandise shipped to their distributors. The only way the restricted offering might have become apparent to a distributor is for their representative to attend the annual Leipzig trade show[15]. Even then, it is unlikely merchandise suitable for the American market would have been displayed at this event[16].

Fortunately, the information described above was recorded in a 1903 trade catalog from the C.E. Wheelock Company. Moreover, it is confirmed by information in trade catalogs from several other firms. A color reproduction of the Wheelock catalog offer is provided in Appendix 7.

The role of trade names in the sale of R.S. Prussia has not been described before. Instead, these names have been associated with second party manufacture[17]. The strong relationship between trade named and RS trademarked merchandise is made quite clear by Gaston. Yet, because the marks are different, it is assumed the origins are different, even though the mold and transfer patterns might be identical. We need to examine the feasibility of the involvement of other parties more closely.

Most of the trade name tableware to be found in the American market appears in this chapter. Overall, the decoration on trade named and trademarked objects is not mutually exclusive. For example, identical transfers appear on objects marked with Saxe Altenburg Germany as well as RS Steeple Germany (red). Further, transfers used on Royal Suhl Germany (red) or Royal Coburg Germany (red) appear also on objects marked with Saxe Altenburg Germany (red). Many different decorating firms would have had to obtain the same R.S. Prussia molds and the same transfers from Reinhold's supplier(s), if different trade names originated with different decorators, and compete in the same marketplace. While we consider this to be an impossibility, we still need ask if it might be allowed by a special set of circumstances.

One special situation, proposed by R. Capers (Capers, 1996), invokes the sale of surplus R.S. Prussia molds and decorating transfers to other firms when the Suhl operation was shut down. We think this improbable for the following reasons. First, there should have been no significant stock of old merchandise, as the firm was constantly producing to order. Second, even if the firm could see the handwriting on the wall and planned as early as 1914 to close Suhl, it is at least eight years later than the time American wholesale firms had **discontinued** all of the mold patterns involved. We can find no evidence for the reappearance of either molds or transfers used on trade name goods[18]. Even more important, Art Nouveau patterns were virtually unsalable after 1909. Butler Bros. found this out with a chocolate set in the Sunflower Mold (RSP Mold 31), first offered by them in 1910 and then repeatedly for the next 6 years. Third, some of the transfers found on trade name goods were used on mold patterns made after 1905, often in combination with newer transfers. We think this is the way the firm used any residual stock of transfer patterns. We show some examples of the later use of transfers in illustrations at the end of this chapter.

In our opinion, the sale of either surplus whiteware, retired mold patterns[19], or unused transfers to competing manufacturers would not be in the best interests of the firm. All of the facts available to us indicate trade names were used to facilitate the sale of merchandise into different avenues of the American market.

For each pattern related to Hidden Image, we first show an example from a trade catalog, if available. Quite often there is a trivial name for the pattern, and we include this information as well. We then illustrate objects marked with trade names or trademarks.

For some patterns, we show objects decorated with transfers other than the Hidden Image type. These examples are included to show the diversity in the decoration of the pattern. However, we purposely try to exclude examples decorated with decals used after 1905.

We begin this section of related molds with the pattern RS 24, first carried by G. Sommers & Co. in 1901, then later by H. Nerlich & Co. in 1902. Upright pieces in this mold appear not to have been made. The embossed rims of many objects are similar to those of the Hidden Image pattern, and are decorated with a transfer of a spider web. The values today for objects in this pattern do not reflect their original, very high wholesale prices.

It was a common practice in the Art Nouveau period to perforate the edges of a mold to enhance a floral pattern. The plain (unperforated) salad bowl in Mold RS 25, illustrated by G. Sommers & Co. in 1901, sold for $16.00 per dozen. When perforated, it was offered by H. Nerlich & Co. for $24 or $30 per dozen, depending upon the decoration. The very high prices, coupled with greater fragility, explain the current scarcity of perforated pieces in the antique marketplace. We are fortunate to be able to show examples matching the descriptions at both price levels in the Nerlich catalog.

Molds RS 25 and RS 26 are similar, but differ by the floral patterns along the rim. Consequently, they are given separate numbers. Mold RS 25 has a mixture of snowdrops and daffodils in the rims, but those of Mold RS 26 just have daffodils.

Mold RS 27, a variation of RSP Mold 343 without the beading along the edge, appears for a brief time in wholesale catalogs beginning in 1902. This is followed by examples of RSP Mold 343. This latter mold is interesting, in view of the large number of trademarks and trade names to be found on this pattern. This mold had a much longer lifetime than most, as objects can be found marked with the classic RS Prussia Wreath. The most prevalent trade names on Mold 343 are Saxe Altenburg Germany (red) and Royal Coburg Germany (red), both printed overglaze. A listing of the decoration associated with each of the trade names found on Mold RSP 343 is provided in Appendix 8. From this list, one can easily see how the decoration used for each trade name was narrowly limited, yet overlapped to a slight extent with others. This overlap shows the decoration subjects were not mutually exclusive, and essentially eliminates the possibility these trade names originated from other firms.

The mug listed as #M1014 by G. Sommers & Co. in 1902 is from a very scarce tableware pattern we designate as Mold RS 30. Cake plates are the most common tableware objects found today, although many other items were originally offered by wholesale firms. To our knowledge, no marks of any kind appear on tableware objects. On the other hand, the elements of this pattern were incorporated into vases of several different shapes (RV Molds 20 and 27) for the Royal Vienna Germany (red) marked decorative line of products shown in Chapter 4.

Two very similar, new patterns for 1902 incorporate either a stylized poppy or pansy in the body of the pattern, attached to rectilinear shaped stems. The easiest way to differentiate the two patterns is to look for a pod in the center of the flowers. The pansy form is designated Mold RS 31, and the poppy form, Mold RS 32. Both of these molds are easily confused with the Modified Iris mold pattern, Steeple Mold 6[20]. To our knowledge, molds RS 31 and RS 32 are not marked with RS Steeple (red) trademarks, but they may be found marked with Saxe Altenburg Germany and Royal Berlin Germany (red) trade names. We have renamed these patterns with RS mold numbers in order to avoid confusion arising from a reference to a specific trade name or trademark. Both patterns were used for a variety of common tableware, and at least two sizes of boxes.

The "Fluted Column" mold pattern, Mold RS 33, was first offered by G. Sommers & Co. in 1902. While this mold was used for a wide variety of upright shaped items, we can find no carryover of mold elements to flat objects. This mold was also included with RS Steeple marked objects (Gaston, 1994), even though trade-marked examples were unknown[21], but no mold number was assigned. Many other wholesale firms carried this pattern.

One of the more popular molds for 1902 is currently known to collectors as the "Modified Iris". Other names are Iris Variation, Steeple Mold 6, and RSP Mold 514. While bowls and cake plates predominate, many other types of objects are shown in trade catalogs. Objects in this mold are known to be marked with the RS Steeple Germany (red) trademark, and the Saxe Altenburg Germany or Royal Hamburg Germany trade names.

Mold patterns produced for the 1903 season seem to be the last to be routinely decorated with Hidden Image type transfers. New patterns for this year include Steeple Mold 12, a pattern used for both flat and upright objects. This mold is distinguished by the extension of the handle of upright objects to meet the foot.

Steeple Mold 3 was carried by many wholesale concerns. Here, large flowers are incorporated into the rim, and they are always decorated as such. In spite of wide distribution, relatively few items were made. Plates, bowls, and trays are common, but upright objects are scarce. This pattern was used for a number of trade names, but Saxe Altenburg Germany is by far the most common. Mold RS 37 is a modification of Steeple Mold 3, made only for the large tray. Here, the side was cut out to accentuate the floral pattern. This is but one of many patterns to be modified by cutting out part of the object while the clay was soft. A similar tray, marked with Saxe Altenburg Germany, is shown by Gaston (Gaston, 1994, Series 4, Plate 490.) The two molds differ by the position of the open flowers.

The popularity of cut glass in the 1900-1905 period likely motivated the Schlegelmilch firm to produce a cut glass pattern, Mold RS 38. Unusual color combinations were used for the decoration, and they accentuate the geometric shapes. We suspect this pattern had a short life, as objects are rarely available in the antique marketplace. No trademarks or trade names are currently known to be to be used in conjunction with this pattern.

Other molds with no corresponding trade references appear next. Mold RS 42, the Picket Fence pattern is only known to be used for salad bowls and berry sets. Both the house and picket fence patterns are recurring themes in R.S. Prussia. Mold RS 44 incorporates an overhanging scroll in the mold, and is one of the few to have flowers projecting out of the surface. We show examples of this pattern decorated with two of only four known Colonial Scenes. Several boxes are known to have this type of flower, but they are quite scarce. Mold RS 43 is a swirl mold with a ragged edge, and is one of the few R.S. Prussia molds to be decorated with a center medallion. If it were not for the Hidden Image decoration, this mold might be thought to be of Austrian origin.

The most complicated R.S. Prussia molds used for tableware are those of double wall construction. There are two types, designated Mold RS 45 and RS 46, owing to the difference in the rim patterns. Very complex floral patterns are cut into the outer wall of upright objects, or the inner wall of plates and bowls. In addition, elaborate embossed designs appear on the back of each item. Few other contemporary molds show such an exquisite embellishment. Occasionally, bright gold was applied behind the cut-out portion to accentuate the floral design. All of the gilded versions of these cut-out objects are exceptionally scarce today.

Individual examples of several mold patterns decorated with Hidden Image transfers are presented next. With the exception of the child's commode set, we have not been able to identify these patterns in trade catalogs. The mold for the commode set first appears in a Butler Bros. 1890 catalog, and several sets with much later decoration are shown in the section of miscellaneous items of *French and German Dolls, Dishes and Accessories*[22].

Molds known to have been produced after 1904, but decorated with Hidden Image transfers, complete Chapter 3. These objects are important for they show left over Hidden Image transfers were used on objects produced well after 1904, rather than sold to other porcelain manufacturing and/or decorating firms when the Suhl manufacturing plant was closed in 1917.

A few of the mold patterns shown in this Chapter include containers with stars molded into the center of the bottom. The number of points, overall size, and shape vary considerably. Stars with four, six, eight, and twelve points are common to R.S.Prussia. Some stars are flat, some are partially segmented, and some are completely segmented. The arms of some stars are even, on others they alternate between two lengths[23]. We have noticed only slight variation in the type of stars on a given mold pattern. Apart from the possibility of their being used to improve structural integrity, we cannot yet assign any significance to star marks.

Endnotes

1. Examples of second quality china may be warped from the firing, or have surface bubbles and/or a fine, dark sand incorporated into the glaze. We have seen Hidden Image salad bowls so warped they cannot be stacked. On most R.S. Prussia objects, one can see where a few surface blemishes have been removed with small grinding wheels. These blemishes were not removed on a large fraction of Hidden Image objects. The incorporation of sand in the glaze was likely the result of a fracture or sloughing of the inside of the sagger used to hold the piece during the glaze firing. Grit of any type is rarely found in the glaze of other R.S. Prussia objects. These seconds are quite distinct from those having been cracked at the glowpaste stage. A large fraction of cracked seconds were subsequently used to make ware with cobalt decoration.

2. Notice the firm already knew in early Spring the merchandise that was to be available in the Fall. This could not have happened unless they had already placed their order with Reinhold's firm.

3. China from both the Oscar and Erdmann Schlegelmilch firms is illustrated in this issue, but no mention is made of a "Schlegelmilch" origin in any of the individual descriptions.

4. The Capers notation for these marks is RS 5.3R 20 and RS 5.3R 6, respectively.

5. The Hidden Image pattern was not the only one to be closed out in 1904. Other items in the "Stippled Floral" mold, and RSP Mold 256, were closed out as either "trademarked Bavarian china", or "trademarked Austrian china". The only marks we know to be used on the Stippled Floral mold are

the classic RS Prussia Wreath, a Crown with "Viersa", and the RS Steeple Germany (gold) trademark.

6. The relative impact the decoration has on the current valuation is also shown by this sequence.

7. Chocolate cup and saucer sets were not routinely sold with the pot in matching decoration until 1904-05. The only chocolate sets we have seen illustrated in trade catalogs were comprised of a pot and six cups and saucers, and the cups/saucer sets were not always in the same mold as the pot.

8. The marks in use (or discontinued) by Reinhold Schlegelmilch are recorded in the various Coburg Directories. Although the RS Steeple is noted as discontinued in the 1913 and 1922 issues, it reappears as current in 1925. Unfortunately, no mention is made of color. Translations of appropriate parts of the Coburg Directories appear in No. 31-32 issues of the *Newsletter of the Int'l Assoc. R.S. Prussia Collectors*.

9. Objects marked with "ambiguous" trade names were not attributed to the R.S. factory by Mary F. Gaston, as the marks had not been "definitely documented" at the time of writing Series 4 of The *Collector's Encyclopedia of R.S. Prussia*, (Gaston, 1995).

10. Other trade names on "trademarked" objects in the 1906 Fall catalog are Royal Hamburg Germany (red) (Capers mark RS 5.3R 6)), Royal Vienna Germany (red), and Royal Baden Made in Germany (red) (Capers mark RS 5.3R 13). Most of the same 1906 catalog cuts can be found in the Fall 1903 issue, where they were described (at higher prices) as (RS) Schlegelmilch china.

11. It is quite possible the packages were marked (to conform to U.S. Customs regulations) rather than the china.

12. Most of the known trade names are listed in *Capers Notes on the Marks of Prussia* (Capers, 1996), under Section 5.3 "Cities-Royal and Otherwise." These are to be distinguished from the retail store logos found in Sections RS 5.1 through 5.2.

13. A discussion of the way German china was sold through American wholesale firms is given in Chapter 4, *R.S. Prussia - The Early Years* (Marple, 1997).

14. Small bottle shape vases are often described as R.S. Prussia salesman samples, particularily in auction catalogs. In general, far too many exist for them to have been used by factory representatives. In addition, many of these pieces have no larger counterparts.

15. The Coburg Directory for 1904 lists trade show participation at Leipzig, and one showroom in Amsterdam.

16. B. Hartwich notes the Reinhold Schlegelmilch firm strictly observed "the national taste of every market country" on p. 31 of *The History of the Suhl Porcelain Factories, 1861-1937*.

17. For the characteristics of china marked with various Royal marks, see also the discussion in Series 4, p. 179 in *Collector's Encyclopedia of R.S. Prussia* (Gaston, 1995).

18. By 1910, R.S. Prussia mold patterns had become very simplified and were devoid of embossed patterns. In our opinion, merchandise made from R.S. molds used between 1902 and 1905 would have been unsalable after 1909.

19. Arguments based on the sale of discontinued molds invariably lose their appeal when accurate mold dating information is taken into account. For example, Capers (Capers, 1996) attributes the blue underglaze "elaborate crown" and Germany mark RS 2.9B 1 to J.S. Kestner Porzellanfabrik with production after 1917. This mark is on an object made from Mold OM 20 and decorated with transfer OT 11. We first see Mold OM 20 in 1896. Decal decorated examples of this mold do appear in 1903 catalog listings. However, the outline transfer OT 11 disappeared from trade catalogs, along with others, after 1900. Consequently, the object marked with the elaborate crown was most likely made before 1901, and certainly before 1903, the last known year Mold OM 20 was produced.

20. For example, the Art Nouveau Daisy mold was incorrectly identified as the Modified Iris on p. 34 of Series 4 by Mary F. Gaston in *Collector's Encyclopedia of R.S. Prussia*, (Gaston, 1995).

21. We assigned a new RS mold number, rather than continuing to use Steeple Mold 16 for this pattern. We think this is appropriate, as the only known trade name to be used on this mold is Saxe Altenburg Germany.

22. R.S. Prussia commode sets in this mold pattern are shown by Doris A. Lechler in Figs. 50, 63-64, (Lechler, 1991).

23. A summary of star mark patterns on R.S. Prussia is presented by Mr. Richard Elliott in issue No. 30 in *The Wreath & Star*, (Ohio Club R.S. Prussia Newsletter, 1995).

K3 216 $0.85

K3 216 Schlegelmilch's 1903 embossed flower design, beautifully tinted and gilded, center decoration of large purple petunias on shaded blue backgrounds with small white blossoms showing through, embossing, edges/ and knob all gold-traced, height over 7 inches. You cannot do a good holiday trade without bright, snappy goods of this kind.   Each, $0.85

Left: Plate 382. Illustration of cracker jar, K3 216 in Hidden Image pattern from Falker and Stern Co. Fall 1903 catalog. Also shown in Butler Bros. Nov. 1903 and G. Sommers & Co. 1901-1904 catalogs. *Courtesy of Amador Collections, Rio Grande Historical Collections, New Mexico State University Library.*

Plate 385. Cake plate, turquoise band in rim, two images, decor HI 7, 11.5" d. This plate was offered as "The Florodora", deep cake plate, deep enough to use for salad, by G. Sommers & Co. in their Fall 1901 catalog. $600-$900.

Plate 383. Cake plate, blue/buff, two images in rim, decor FD F, 11.5" d. This is the only object we have seen to be decorated with a transfer used on RS Steeple Germany marked ware. $400-$600.

Plate 386. Cake plate, pink band in rim, two images, decor HI 3, 11.5" d. $600-$900

Plate 384. Cake plate, blue shades, two images, decor HI 5, 11.5" d. $600-$900.

Plate 387. Cake plate, fuchsia rim, two images, gold overlay on hair, decor HI 2, 11.5" d. $900-$1300.

Plate 388. Cake plate, pink, two images in rim medallions, decor HI 3, 11.5" d. $1300-1800.

Plate 389. Cake plate, buff/cobalt, two images, decor HI 9, 11.5" d. $1300-$1800.

Plate 390. Cake plate, light green, single image in rim, decor HI 5, 10.5" d. $400-$600.

Right: Plate 393. Cake plate, emerald green, single image in rim medallion, decor HI 3, 9.5" d. $600-$900.

Plate 391. Cake plate, light pink, single image, decor HI 8, 10.5" d. $250-$400.

Right: Plate 394. Cake plate, deep blue, single image in rim medallion, decor HI 2, 9.5" d. Marked Royal Hamburg Germany (red). $600-$900.

Plate 392. Cake plate, buff/ green, single image with outline transfer hair, decor HI 14, 10.5" d. $400-$600.

Right: Plate 395. Cake plate, buff/cobalt, single image, decor HI 9, 9.5" d. $600-$900.

Left: Plate 396. Plate, light blue, single image in rim, decor HI 5, 9" d. $250-$400.

Left: Plate 397. Plate, light green rim, girl with hat facing front, decor HI 6, 10.5" d. $250-$400.

Plate 399. Bowl, blue/cobalt, single image in cobalt rim medallion, decor HI 1, 10" d. $600-$900.

Left: Plate 398. Bowl, peacock green rim, single image in gold rim medallion, decor HI 4, 10" d. $600-$900.

Plate 400. Bowl, turquoise rim, single image in rim with gold overlay on hair, decor HI 7, 10" d.

Plate 403. Bowl, shaded blue rim, single image in rim, decor HI 14, 7.5" d. $150-$250.

Plate 401. Bowl, turquoise rim, single image in rim with gold overlay on hair, decor HI 2, 9" d. $400-$600.

Plate 404. Bowl, deep green, single image in blue/purple medallion, decor HI 3, 7.5" d. Marked Royal Hamburg Germany (red). $250-$400.

Plate 402. Bowl, light blue rim band, single image in rim, decor HI 7, 7.5" d. $150-$250.

Plate 405. Bowl, buff/cobalt, single image in rim, decor HI 2, 6.5" d. $250-$400.

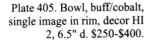

96

Plate 406. Handled bowl, Tiffany bronze rim, single image in gold medallion of handle, decor HI 4, 12" l. $1300-$1800.

Plate 408. Handled bowl, blue/cobalt, single image in cobalt medallion of handle, decor HI 1, 12" l. $2500++.

Plate 409. Celery tray, light blue, single image in rim, decor HI 7, 12.25" l. $150-$250.

Plate 407. Handled bowl, strong pink background, single image in blue medallion of handle, decor HI 3, 12" l. Marked Saxe Altenburg Germany (red). $1300-$1800.

Plate 410. Celery tray, peacock green edge, single image in rim, decor HI 4, 12.25" l. $400-$600.

Plate 411. Relish tray, green/ buff, single image in rim, decor HI 14, 8.75" l. $150-$250.

Plate 412. Lemonade pitcher, shaded maroon/buff, images on front and back of body, decor HI 2, 9" h. $1800-$2500.

Plate 414. Lemonade pitcher, reverse of Plate 412.

Plate 413. Lemonade pitcher, shaded green/buff, two images in body, decor HI 2, 9" h. $1300-$1800.

Plate 415. Water pitcher, lavender/buff, images on both sides of body, 7.5" h. $1300-$1800.

Plate 416. Milk pitcher, shades of green, single image in body, decor HI 5, 6.25" h. Very scarce size. $400-$600.

Plate 419. Cream pitcher, single image, decor HI 5, 3.25" h. $150-$250.

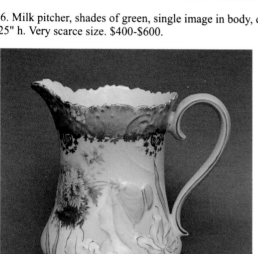

Plate 417. Milk pitcher, green band at top, single image, decor HI 2, 6.25" h. $400-$600.

Plate 420. Cream pitcher, single image, decor HI 2, 3.25" h. $150-$250.

Plate 418. Pitcher, white, single image, decor HI 3, 4.5" h. $150-$250.

Plate 421. Sugar bowl, single image, decor HI 5, 4.25" h. $150-$250.

Plate 422. Syrup pitcher with underplate, green band at top, decor HI 2, pitcher 4.5" h., saucer 5.5" d. $400-$600.

Plate 424. Chocolate pot, shades of lavender, decor HI 2, 9" h. Scarce color. $1300-$1800.

Plate 423. Chocolate pot, green band at top, two images on opposite sides, decor HI 2, 9" h. $600-$900.

Plate 425. Chocolate set, decor HI 2, pot 9" h., cups 2.75" h., saucers 4" d. $2500++

Right: Plate 426. Teapot, green rim, single image, decor HI 2, 5.37" h. $600-$900.

Plate 430. Half-size moustache cup, pink at top, single image, decor HI 10, 2.5" h. Catalog illustrations show Hidden Image mugs were sold without matching saucers. $250-$400.

Plate 427. Teapot, blue, single image, decor HI 5, 5.37" h. $600-$900.

Left: Plate 431. Mug, green at top, single image with outline transfer on hair, decor HI 5, 3.5" h. $250-$400.

Plate 428. Mustard pot, light green, decor HI 2, 3.75" h. $250-$400.

Left: Plate 429. Cracker jar, dark green at top, two images on opposite sides, only one with gold overlay on hair, decor HI 3, 7.25" h. $900-$1300.

Plate 432. Shaving mug, pink band at top, decor HI 7, 3.5" h. $250-$400.

Plate 433. Dresser tray, blue, two images in rim, decor HI 6, 11" l., 7.25" w. $250-$400.

Plate 436. Tray, green background, decor HI 3, 6.5" l., 4.75" w. $600-$900.

Plate 434. Dresser tray, green, two images, decor HI 2, 11" l, 7.25" w. $400-$600.

Plate 437. Tray, white, decor HI 3, 6" l, 4" w. $400-$600.

Plate 435. Tray, white, decor HI 3, 6.25" l., 4.5" w. $600-$900.

Right: Plate 438. Tray, white, image in bottom of tray, two loops at bottom of tray, 7" l., 5" w. $400-$600.

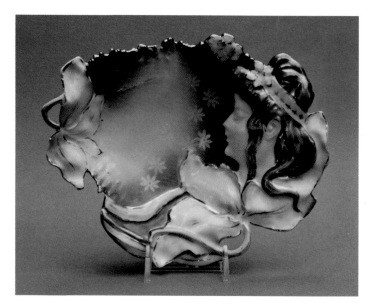

Plate 439. Tray, green background, decor HI 3, 5.5" l., 4.75" w. The identical tray was offered by G. Sommers & Co. in the 1902 Holiday issue with the note "cannot fail to be a ready seller". Price, $2.50 per dozen. $250-$400.

Plate 442. Tray, green/purple, image with gold overlay on hair, 7" l., 5.5" w. $900-$1300.

Plate 440. Tray, light green background, decor HI 6, 7.25" l, 6" w. $400-$600.

Plate 441. Tray, white, decor HI 3, 7.25" l., 6" w. $400-$600.

Plate 443. Tray, white, decor HI 3, 6.75" l., 5.5" w. $250-$400.

Plate 444. Hairpin box, turquoise, hairpin embossed on lid, decor HI 7, 4.75" l., 2.75" w. $400-$600.

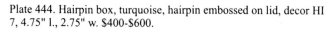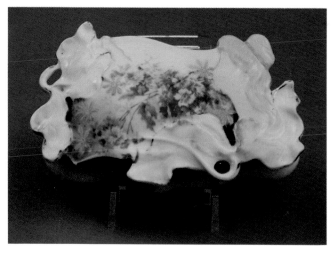

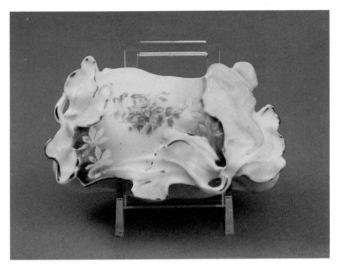

Plate 445. Match box (striker under lid), decor HI 11, 4.75" l., 2.75" w. $400-$600.

Plate 448. Box, white, decor HI 3, 6.5" l., 4.75" w. Loop at bottom has been repaired. $400-$600.

Plate 446. Box, white, decor HI 3, 5" l., 4" w. $400-$600.

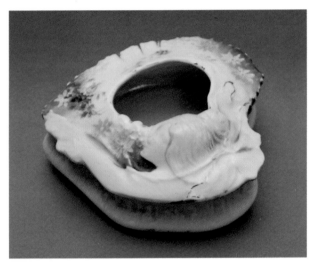

Plate 449. Hair receiver, white, decor HI 13, 4.5" l., 4" w. $250-$400.

Plate 447. Box, light pink, decor HI 5, 6.25" l., 4.25" w. $400-$600.

Plate 450. Hair receiver, magenta rim, gold overlay on hair, 4.5" l., 4" w. $400-$600.

Left: Plate 451. Toothpick holder, green, decor HI 2, 2.25" h. $400-$600.

No. 3/209. $21.00 dozen.

3/209. Diameter 10¼ inches, fancy fluted shape, crimped outer rim, clouded gold edge tinted border, gold work insertion effect, color band and inner margin of gold lacework, assorted rich floral centres........................ 21 00

No. 3/210. $24.00 dozen.

3/210. Diameter 10¼ inches, beaded gold edge, elaborately embossed in gold rim and floral panel effect, gold garland at foot of panels, assorted floral designs in centre.............. 24 00

3/266. Diameter 10¼ inches, beaded gold edge, beautiful royal blue tint with Bermuda lily decoration in centre outlined in raised gold, gold fern border inside top edge with gold stars and gold leaf decoration..................... 30 00

Plate 454. Illustration of salad bowl 3/209 in Mold RS 24, 3/210 (and 3/266) in Mold RS 25 from Nerlich & Co. Spring 1903 catalog. Also shown is the salad bowl in Mold RS 25. Pattern RS 24 also illustrated in G. Sommers & Co. Fall 1901 catalog. *Courtesy of the National Library of Canada.*

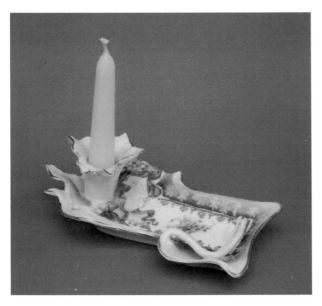

Plate 452. Candle holder, green edge, outline transfer on hair, decor HI 13, 6" l., 3.25" w. $900-$1300.

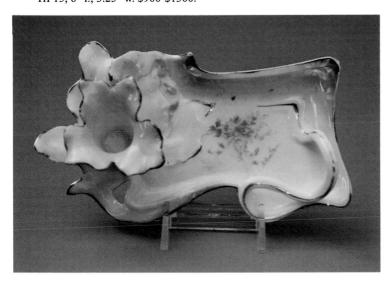

Plate 453. Candle holder, light blue, decor HI 13, 6" l., 3.25" w. $900-$1300.

Plate 455. Individual cake plate, purple rim, Mold RS 24, decor HI 3, 6" d. Marked Royal Oldenburg made in Germany. Under $50.

Plate 456. Cake plate, turquoise rim, Mold RS 24, decor HI 2, 11.75" d. $75-$100.

Plate 458. Bowl, ochre rim, Mold RS 24, decor HI 3, 9" d. $50-$75.

Plate 457. Cake plate, ochre rim, Mold RS 24, pink/yellow rose decor, 9.5" d. Royal Dresden made in Germany. $50-$75.

Plate 459. Salad bowl, buff rim, Mold RS 25, decor HI 2, 10.25" d. $150-$250.

Right: Plate 460. Salad bowl, buff/white rim, Mold RS 25, decor HI 9, 10" d. This bowl has a perforated rim as shown in the Nerlich catalog illustration. $250-$400.

Plate 462. Charger, red rim, variation of Mold RS 25, decor HI 3, 12" d. $250-$400.

Left: Plate 461. Salad bowl, turquoise rim, Mold RS 25, decor HI 3, 10.25" d. Rim is only partially cut away. $150-$250.

Plate 464. Cake plate, red rim, variation of Mold RS 25, pink/yellow rose decor, 10" d. While common on related molds, this decal was not used on Hidden Image. Marked Royal Dresden made in Germany. $250-$400.

Plate 465. Cake plate, buff rim, variation of Mold RS 25, decor HI 2, 10.25" d. $250-400

Left: Plate 463. Small plate, cobalt rim, variation of Mold RS 26, decor HI 2, 8.5" d. Marked with Viersa and crown. $150-$250.

Plate 466. Celery tray, buff rim, variation of Mold RS 25, multi-floral transfer, 12.25" l. $250-$400.

Plate 467. Illustration of four piece table set 3/217 in Mold RS 27 from Nerlich & Co. Spring 1903 catalog. Also shown in G. Sommers & Co. Fall 1901 catalog. *Courtesy of the National Library of Canada.*

No. 3,217. $2.30 per set.   Per Set

3/217 Fancy colored border ornamented in white, rich flower decoration and fern sprays of gold, assorted blue and green tint borders $2 30
3/218. Same shape as 3/217, assorted blue and green tints, very rich decoration in gold and flowers.   2 80

Plate 468. Cake plate, red rim, Mold RS 27, center medallion, 11.12" d. $75-$100.

Plate 469. Cake plate, green rim, Mold RS 27, decor HI 3, 9.62" d. $50-$75.

Plate 470. Syrup pitcher, blue rim, Mold RS 27, decor HI 3, 4.25" h. Complete set (with underplate) $100-$150.

108

Plate 471. Mustard pot, pink rim, Mold RS 27, decor HI 3, 3.12" h. $75-$100.

Plate 474. Three piece tea set, blue rim, Mold RS 27, Courting scene transfers, tea pot 4.75" h., sugar 3.75" h., cream 3" h. $250-$400.

Plate 472. Relish tray, green rim, Mold RS 27, decor HI 14, 9.5" l., 4.5" w. $50-$75.

A16. Floral Decorated. Fancy shape, fine china, gold traced scalloped edge, body tinted in variegated shades of blue and old ivory, handsomely decorated with large clusters of beautiful flowers in natural colors, enamel effect, floral ornamentations over tinted ground on rim, cover with gold decorated handle to match; size 4¾ x 7½ inches, beautiful in design and finish, 1-6 dozen in pkg; per doz.............. 9.00

A16, $9.00 per doz.

Plate 475. Illustration of cracker jar A16 in RSP Mold 343 from Webb-Freyschlag Sept. 1903 catalog. *Courtesy of Amador Collections, Rio Grande Historical Collections, New Mexico State University Library.*

Plate 473. Bun tray, pink rim, Mold RS 27, decor HI 3, 12.37" l., 8" w. $75-$100.

Plate 476. Charger, cobalt rim with white flowers, RSP Mold 343, Lady with Fan decor, 12." d. $1800-$2500.

Plate 477. Cake plate, peacock blue rim, RSP Mold 343, decor HI 1 with Allegorical scenes in reserves, 11.25" d. $250-$400.

Plate 479. Small plate, cobalt, RSP Mold 343, daffodil decor, 9" d. $250-$400.

Plate 480. Small plate, cobalt rim, RSP Mold 343, decor HI 4, 9" d. Marked Saxe Altenburg Germany. $100-$150.

Plate 478. Small plate, luster green rim, RSP Mold 343, decor HI 2, 9" d. Marked Saxe Altenburg Germany with crown (red). $50-$75.

Right: Plate 481. Small plate, peacock blue rim, RSP Mold 343, decor HI 1 with cupids series 1 in reserves, 6.5" d. $100-$150.

Left: Plate 482. Small plate, peacock blue rim, RSP Mold 343, decor HI ! with cupids series 1 in reserves, 6.5" d. $100-$150.

Left: Plate 483. Salad bowl, cobalt rim, RSP Mold 343, decor same series as P 2, Allegorical scenes in white band, 10.25" d. $100-$150.

Plate 485. Salad bowl, cobalt rim with white flower, RSP Mold 343, pink rose decor, 10" d. Marked RS Steeple Germany (red). $250-$400.

Left: Plate 484. Small bowl, cobalt rim, RSP Mold 343, yellow roses decor, 9" d. Marked with Viersa and crown (red). $150-$250.

Plate 486. Salad bowl, peacock blue rim, RSP Mold 343, Diana the Huntress with cupids series 1 in reserves, 10" d. $400-$600.

Plate 487. Small bowl, peacock blue rim, RSP Mold 343, decor HI 1 with Allegorical scenes in reserves, 9" d. $150-$250.

Plate 490. Chocolate pot, cobalt, RSP Mold 343, daffodil decor, 9.25" h. Marked Royal Coburg Germany with crown. $900-$1300.

Plate 488. Small bowl, pink rim with spiderweb overlay, RSP Mold 343, pink/yellow roses decor, 9" d. $50-$75.

Plate 491. Mush and milk set, greens, RSP Mold 343, decor HI 3, pitcher 3.25" h., bowl 5.5" d., plate 7" d. $100-$150.

Plate 489. Tea cup/saucer set, green cup rim, RSP Mold 343, decor HI 4, cup 2.62" h., saucer 5.5" d. $50-$75.

Right: Plate 492. Cracker jar, green rim, RSP Mold 343, decor HI 5, 7.75" h. $100-$150.

Plate 493. Tray, peacock blue rim, RSP Mold 343, decor HI 5 with cupids series 1 in white band, 11.5" l. $150-$250.

M 1014—Novel and very beautiful mug for shaving or drinking; swell shape; beautiful floral decoration; fancy luster handle; fancy edges in assorted iridescent colored lusters 4.00

M 1014. $4.00 Doz.

Plate 494. Illustration of china mug M 1014 in Mold RS 30 from G. Sommers & Co. Holiday 1902 catalog. Also shown in Sommers & Co. 1903-1904, and Butler Bros. Nov. 1903 and 1904 catalogs. *Courtesy of Minnesota Historical Society Library.*

Plate 495. Cake plate, buff rim, Mold RS 30, decor HI 5, 11" d. $75-$100.

Plate 496. Cake plate, cobalt, Mold RS 30, decor HI 4, 10.5" d. $250-$400.

K3 280. Schlegelmilch china, embossed leaf and flower border all traced out in gold, rich mottled dark green, pink and cream ground, lavishly decorated with beautiful purple petunias, gold traced open handles and edges, diameter 10½. We sell you this rich Schlegelmilch china so cheap that you can easily double your money. Ea., $0.85

Plate 497. Illustration of cake plate K3 280 in Mold RS 31 (Art Nouveau Pansy) from Falker and Stern Co. Fall 1903 catalog. Objects in this pattern were closed out in 1906. Also shown in G. Sommers & Co. 1902-1904 catalogs. *Courtesy of Amador Collections, Rio Grande Historical Collections, New Mexico State University Library.*

Plate 498. Salad bowl, buff rim with cobalt center, Mold RS 31, small floral decor, 10" d. Marked Royal Berlin Germany. $250-$400.

Plate 500. Cake plate, pink, Mold RS 31, decor HI 3, 10.5" d. $150-$250.

Plate 499. Cake plate, buff rim with cobalt center, Mold RS 31, small floral decor, 10.75" d. Marked Saxe Altenburg Germany. $250-$400.

Right: Plate 501. Three piece tea set, blue edges, Mold RS 31, decor HI 2, tea pot 6.25" h., sugar 5.25" h., cream 4.5" h. $150-$250.

Left: Plate 502. Chocolate pot, brown top edge, Mold RS 31, decor HI 1, 9.5" h. $250-$400.

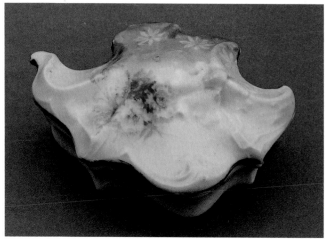

Plate 505. Box, green/buff rim, Mold RS 32, pink rose decor, 4" l., 3.75" w. $50-$75.

Plate 503. Serving tray, blue rim, Mold RS 32, decor HI 4, 11.5" l, 7" w. $100-$150.

Plate 506. Box, green/buff top, Mold RS 32, decor HI 2, 4" l. $75-$100.

Left: Plate 504. Cake plate, green/buff rim, Mold RS 32, decor HI 1, 11" d. $75-$100.

Right: Plate 509. Cake plate, green edge, Mold RS 29, decor HI 1, 10.75" d. Marked Saxe Altenburg Germany. $75-$100.

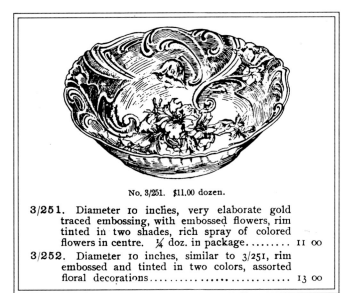

No. 3/251. $11.00 dozen.

3/251. Diameter 10 inches, very elaborate gold traced embossing, with embossed flowers, rim tinted in two shades, rich spray of colored flowers in centre. ¼ doz. in package......... 11 00

3/252. Diameter 10 inches, similar to 3/251, rim embossed and tinted in two colors, assorted floral decorations............................ 13 00

Plate 507. Illustration of salad bowl, 3/251 (and 3/252), in Mold RS 29 from Nerlich & Co. Spring 1903 catalog. Salad bowls in this mold were closed out by Falker and Stern Co. in 1906. *Courtesy of the National Library of Canada.*

Plate 510. Salad bowl, brown edge, Mold RS 29, decor HI 1, 10.5" d. $50-$75.

Plate 508. Cake plate, bronze edge, Mold RS 29, decor HI 1, 11.25" d. $100-$150.

Right: Plate 511. Salad bowl, green edge, Mold RS 29, decor HI 4, 10.5" d. $75-$100.

116

Plate 512. Illustration of cream/sugar set K3 328 in Mold RS 33 from Falker and Stern Co. Fall 1903 catalog. Also shown in Butler Bros. Nov. 1903-1904, and G. Sommers & Co. 1902 catalogs. *Courtesy of Amador Collections, Rio Grande Historical Collections, New Mexico State University Library.*

K3 328. Schlegel-milch's stylish footed design, richly decorated with floral transfers on shaded backgrounds with white blossoms showing through, handles perforated and gold-traced, edges and feet finished in gold. Capacity of creamer nearly ½ pint, sugar 4½ inches high. 3 sets in pkg., asst'd blue, chocolate and green tints. **Per set, $0.50**

Plate 515. Sugar/cream set, orange top, Mold RS 33, pansy decor, sugar 4.5" h., cream 4.25" h. $150-$250.

Plate 513. Cracker jar, blue, Mold RS 33, decor HI 2, 7.5" h. $150-$250.

Plate 514. Teapot (catalog description), Mold RS 33, decor HI 13, 7" h. Marked Saxe Altenburg Germany. $150-$250.

Plate 516. Chocolate pot, Mold RS 33, decor HI 3 and 13, 9.25" h. $250-$400.

Right: Plate 519. Cake plate (without open handles), cobalt rim, RS Steeple Mold 6, decor HI 4, 11" d. $400-$600.

Plate 517. Illustration mush and milk set K3 204 in RS Steeple Mold 6 from Falker and Stern Co. Fall 1903 catalog. Also shown in Butler Bros. Fall 1903-1904, and G. Sommers & Co. 1902-1904 catalogs. *Courtesy of Aador Collections, Rio Grande Historical Collections, New Mexico State University Library.*

Right: Plate 520. Cake plate, red rim, RS Steeple Mold 6, pink floral decor, 11" d. $250-$400.

Plate 518. Cake plate, green rim, RS Steeple Mold 6, tulips decor, 10.5" d. Marked RS Steeple Germany (red). $250-$400.

Right: Plate 521. Salad bowl, gold rim, RS Steeple Mold 6, multi-floral decor, 10.5" d. $250-$400.

Plate 522. Salad bowl, red rim, RS Steeple Mold 6, pink floral decor, 10.5" d. $250-$400.

Plate 525. Covered box, green rim, RS Steeple Mold 6, small roses decor, 4.25" l. $100-$150.

Plate 523. Salad bowl, irridescent red and peacock blue border, RS Steeple Mold 6, yellow roses decor, 9" d. Marked RS Steeple Germany (red). $250-$400.

Plate 526. Bun tray, bronze Moire rim, RS Steeple Mold 6, tulips decor, 13.5" l., 7.25" w. $250-$400.

Plate 524. Shaving mug with mirror, RS Steeple Mold 6, pink rose decor, 3" h. $150-$250.

A81. Artistic Design. Decorated with clusters of roses, enamel and cameo effect, flowers over light blue tinted ground, scalloped top, wide band and fancy embellishments in solid gold on rim tinted ribbon handle heavy gold traced, size of jug 3⅝x3⅝ inches, oblong sugar 4x3⅜x3⅞ inches, extra fine china, very beautiful; you should have these; ¼ doz in package; per doz...10.⁶⁰

A81, $10.50 per set.

Plate 527. Illustration of low-form sugar/cream set A 81 in RS Steeple Mold 12 from Webb-Freyschlage Sept. 1903 catalog. The three piece tea set with tall-form sugar/cream set was sold as #33. Also shown in Butler Bros. Spring 1903, and G. Sommer & Co. Fall 1902 catalogs. *Courtesy of Amador Collections, Rio Grande Historical Collections, New Mexico State University Library.*

Plate 528. Small plate, pink/buff rim, RS Steeple Mold 12, decor HI 6, 7.5" d. Under $50.

Plate 529. Small footed bowl, peacock blue rim, RS Steeple Mold 12, decor HI 1 with cupids series 1 in reserves, 7.25" d. $250-$400.

Plate 531. Three piece tea set, pink, RS Steeple Mold 12, decor HI 5, pot 5.5" h., sugar 4.5" h., cream 3.5" h. $400-$600.

Plate 530. Cream/sugar set, pink, RS Steeple Mold 12, decor HI 5, sugar 6.5" h., cream 5.37" h. Marked Saxe Altenburg Germany. $250-$400.

Plate 532. Covered box, buff edge on lid, RS Steeple Mold 12, decor HI 3, 3.12" d. Marked Saxe Altenburg Germany. $100-$150.

Plate 533. Cracker jar, pink, RS Steeple Mold 12, decor HI 5, 8" h. $400-$600.

Plate 534. Mustard pot, pink edges, RS Steeple Mold 12, small flower decor, 4.5" h. $250-$400.

Plate 535. Demitasse pot, yellow top, RS Steeple Mold 12, pansy decor, 8" h. $600-$900.

K3 39.
Fine china, made by the renowned Schlegelmilch, has embossed border of leaves, flowers and scrolls splendidly tinted and slashed with gold, large floral transfers in rich colors on shaded tinted ground with white blossoms showing through, dimensions 2¾x9¾. 1-6 doz. asst'd in pkg. A "work of art" and a genuine bargain at $1.00 retail. **Each, $0.59**

Plate 536. Illustration of salad bowl K3 39 in RS Steeple Mold 3 from Falker and Stern Co. Fall 1903 catalog. Closed out by the firm in Fall 1906 catalog. Also shown in Butler Bros. Nov. 1903-1904, and C.E. Wheelock 1903 catalogs. *Courtesy of Amador Collections, Rio Grande Historical Collections, New Mexico State University Library.*

Plate 537. Cake plate, red rim, RS Steeple Mold 3, tulips decor, 10.5" d. Marked RS Steeple Germany (red). $150-$250.

Plate 540. Cake plate, Cobalt rim,
RS Steeple Mold 3, decor HI 5,
9.75" d. $150-$250.

Plate 538. Plate, cobalt, RS Steeple Mold 3, daffodil decor, 9" d.
Marked Saxe Altenburg Germany. $250-$400.

Plate 541. Plate, RS Steeple Mold 3, decor HI 1, 9" d. Marked Saxe
Altenburg Germany. $75-$100.

Plate 539. Cake plate, white rim, RS Steeple Mold 3, decor HI 1 with
Allegorical scenes in reserves, 10.5" d. $250-$400.

Plate 542. Salad bowl, cobalt rim, RS
Steeple Mold 3, decor similar to HI 5,
10.5" d. Marked Saxe Altenburg
Germany. $250-$400.

Left: Plate 543. Salad bowl, gold rim, RS Steeple Mold 3, multi-flower decor, 9" d. Marked RS Steeple Germany (red). $250-$400.

Plate 546. Fancy tray, blue flowers in edge, RS Steeple Mold 3, strawflower decor, 11.5" l., 7" w. $50-$75.

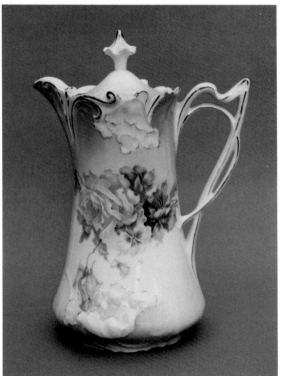

Left: Plate 544. Chocolate pot, pink top, RS Steeple Mold 3, decor HI 5, 9.5" h. $150-$250.

Left: Plate 545. Bun tray, pink edge, RS Steeple Mold 3, decor HI 4, 12.5" l, 8" w. Marked Saxe Altenburg Germany. $150-$250.

Plate 547. Syrup set, green, RS Steeple Mold 3, decor HI 14, syrup 5" h., saucer 5.12" d. Marked Saxe Altenburg Germany. $150-$250.

123

Plate 548. Three piece tea set, RS Steeple Mold 3, decor HI 13 with cupids series 1 in reserves, pot 6.25" h., sugar 5" h., pitcher 4" h. $600-$900.

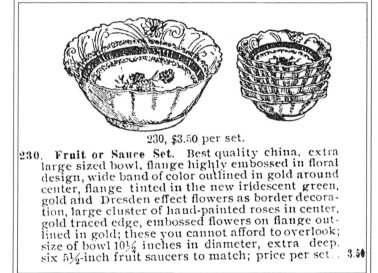

230, $3.50 per set.

230. **Fruit or Sauce Set.** Best quality china, extra large sized bowl, flange highly embossed in floral design, wide band of color outlined in gold around center, flange tinted in the new iridescent green, gold and Dresden effect flowers as border decoration, large cluster of hand-painted roses in center, gold traced edge, embossed flowers on flange outlined in gold; these you cannot afford to overlook; size of bowl 10½ inches in diameter, extra deep, six 5½-inch fruit saucers to match; price per set.. 3.50

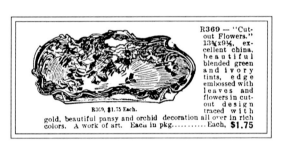

R369 — "Cut-out Flowers." 13¾x9¼, excellent china, beautiful blended green and ivory tints, edge embossed with leaves and flowers in cut-out design traced with gold, beautiful pansy and orchid decoration all over in rich colors. A work of art. Each in pkg...........Each, **$1.75**

R369, $1.75 Each.

Plate 549. Illustration of large tray with "Cut-out Flowers", R369, from Butler Bros. Nov. 1903 catalog. *Courtesy of the New York State Library.*

Plate 551. Illustration of "Fruit or Sauce Set" 230 in Mold RS 40 from Webb-Freyschlag Sept. 1903 catalog. *Courtesy of Aador Collections, Rio Grande Historical Collections, New Mexico State University Library.*

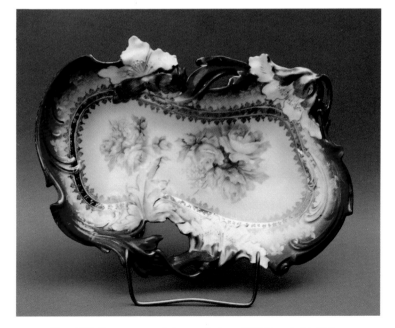

Plate 550. Fancy tray, red rim, variation of RS Steeple Mold 3, yellow roses decor, about 12.75" l., 9.75" w. $600-$900.

Plate 552. Salad bowl, Mold RS 40, decor HI 3, 10.25" d. Marked Royal Baden made in Germany. $75-$100.

Plate 554. Fancy shape salad bowl, cobalt, Mold RS 37, daffodil decor, about 10.75" d. $250-$400.

Left: Plate 553. Salad bowl, peacock blue rim, Mold RS 40, decor HI 4, 10.5" d. $150-$250.

Plate 556. Cake plate, Mold RS 38 (cut glass), decor HI 9, 10" d. $150-$250.

Plate 557. Cake plate, Mold RS 38, decor HI 2, 10" d. $150-$250.

Left: Plate 555. Fancy shape salad bowl, bronze luster rim, Mold RS 37, decor HI 1 with Allegorical Scenes in reserves, about 10.75" d. $150-$250.

Plate 558. Sugar/cream set, green top/bottom, Mold RS 38, sugar decor HI 10, cream decor HI 6, sugar 4.75" h., cream 3.5" h. $100-$150.

Plate 559. Teapot, green/buff, Mold RS 38, pot 5" h. Scarce object. $250-$400.

Plate 560. Shaving mug, lavender/buff, Mold RS 38, decor HI 9, 3.5" h. $150-$250.

Plate 562. Footed salad bowl, Mold RS 41, decor HI 4, 10" d. $100-$150.

Left: Plate 563. Footed salad bowl, buff rim, Mold RS 41, decor HI 3, 10" d. $75-$100.

Left: Plate 564. Salad bowl, pink rim, Mold RS 42 (picket fence), decor HI 7, 10.25" d. $100-$150.

Plate 566. Fancy salad bowl, chocolate/blue rim, Mold RS 44 (overhanging scroll), Courting scene decor, 10.75" d. $1300-$1800.

Left: Plate 565. Salad bowl, blue rim, Mold RS 42, decor HI 3, 10.25" d. $100-$150.

Plate 567. Fancy salad bowl, chocolate/blue rim, Mold RS 44 (overhanging scroll), Courting scene decor, 10.75" d. $1300-$1800.

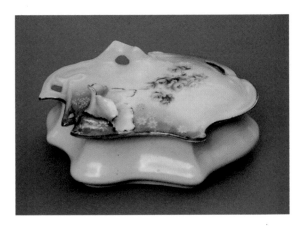

Plate 570. Lidded box, variation Mold RS 44, decor HI 11, 5" l, 4" w. $250-$400.

Plate 568. Fancy salad bowl, buff rim, Mold RS 44, decor HI 3, 10.75" d. $600-$900.

Plate 571. Salad bowl, green rim, Mold RS 43, decor HI 2, 10.5" d. $75-$100.

Plate 569. Fancy salad bowl, buff/green rim, Mold RS 44, pink rose decor, 10.75" d. $250-$400.

Right: Plate 572. Salad bowl, red rim, Mold RS 43, unusual red center medallion, 10.5" d. $75-$100.

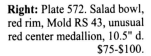

Plate 574. Salad bowl, blue/buff rim, Mold RS 43, Courting scenes in reserves, 10.5" d. $100-$150.

Left : Plate 573. Salad bowl, chocolate/buff rim, Mold RS 43, decor HI 2, 10.5" d. $75-$100.

Plate 576. Large cake plate, pink rim, Mold RS 45, decor HI 6, 11.75" d. $250-$400.

Plate 577. Cake plate, blue rim, Mold RS 45, decor HI 2 with gold behind perforated design, 10" d. $400-$600.

Left: Plate 575. Large cake plate, white rim, Mold RS 45, pink rose decor with gold behind perforated design, 11.75" d. $600-$900.

Plate 580. Salad bowl, blue/buff rim, Mold RS 46, decor HI 3 with gold behind perforated design, 10" d. $400-$600.

Left: Plate 578. Small plate, blue rim, Mold RS 45, decor HI 6, 6" d. $100-$150.

Plate 581. Large cake plate with two types of cut out patterns, pink rim, Mold RS 46, decor HI 10, 12" d. $250-$400.

Plate 579. Oval tray, red rim, Mold RS 45, pink rose decor with gold behind perforated design, 13.5" l., 7.62" w. $400-$600.

Plate 582. Covered sugar or box, pink edges, Mold RS 46, decor HI 6, 3" h., 4.75" l., 3" w. $150-$250.

Plate 583. Syrup pitcher, blue edges, Mold RS 46, decor HI 3, 4.75" h. Complete set (with underplate), $400-$600.

Plate 586. Chocolate pot, blue edges, Mold RS 46, pink rose decor with gold behind perforated design, 9.25" h. $900-$1300.

Plate 584. Shaving mug, green edge, Mold RS 46, decor HI 7 with gold behind perforated design, 3.5" h. $250-$400.

Plate 585. Three piece tea set, green edges, Mold RS 46, decor HI 3, pot 5.5" h., sugar 4.25" h., pitcher 3.25" h. $600-$900.

Plate 587. Spoon holder, blue edge, Mold RS 46, decor HI 10, 4.25" h. $150-$250.

Plate 590. Handled bowl, blue/buff edge, Mold RS 46, Courting scene decor with gold behind perforated design in handle, 11" l. $900-$1300.

Plate 588. Handled basket, green edge, Mold RS 45, decor HI 13, 6" h. $150-$250.

Plate 589. Handled basket, pink edge, Mold RS 45, decor HI 13, 6" h. $150-$250.

Plate 591. Handled bowl, pink edge, Mold RS 46, decor HI 10, 11" l. $400-$600.

Left: Plate 592. Chocolate pot, pink edges, decor HI 1, 9.25" h. $250-$400.

Plate 595. Hexagon shape salad bowl, buff inside, pink outside edge, decor HI 5, 9.5" d. $100-$150.

Plate 593. Salad bowl, pink edge, decor HI 4 with perforated edge, 10" d. $150-$250.

Plate 596. Fancy tray, green edge, decor HI 2, 10.75" l. $75-$100.

Left: Plate 594. Cake plate, buff edge, decor HI 3, 9.5" d. $75-$100.

Plate 597. Cake plate, pink/buff edge, decor HI 3, 10.5" d. $50-$75.

Plate 599. Cream pitcher, RSP Mold 632 (new for 1905), decor HI 2, 3.5" h. Marked classic RS Prussia Wreath. Under $50.

Plate 598. Toy chamber set (in original box), blue edges, decor HI 2, pitcher 6" h., bowl 5.5" d., pot 2.25" h., toothbrush 3.5" l., soap 2.25" w., box 10.75" w. x 14.5" l. $1300-$1800.

Plate 600. Salad bowl, decor HI 5 and blackberries, 11" d. Marked classic RS Germany (green). $100-$150.

Plate 602. Deep tray, cobalt rim, RSP Mold 82 (new for 1906), decor HI 3, 8" l., 6" w. $150-$250.

Plate 601. Cake plate, buff rim, mold not numbered (new for 1906), decor HI 5, 9.62" d. $75-$100.

Plate 603. Toothpick holder, decor HI 9, 2.25" h. Mold very similar to those produced 1908-1909. $75-$100

Chapter Four
Royal Vienna Germany and Related Trade Names

Between 1900 and 1905, the Reinhold Schlegelmilch firm developed and marketed exceptional product lines of ewers, vases, and urns, all in characteristic Art Nouveau forms. Flower forms merge into or protrude from sides, and their stems often form handles. Cobalt and peacock blue, brilliant orange, iridescent and satin metallic colors are commonplace. The porcelain is exceptionally white, very thin, and objects are free of burn spots and other surface blemishes. Fortunately, these objects are generally decorated with the same printed transfers (decals) used on R.S. Prussia tableware. This was our first solid evidence the Royal Vienna Germany trade name should be included as part of R.S. Prussia. We now recognize many trade names were used for decorative items. However, the most common are Royal Vienna (plus crown), Royal Coburg, Saxe Altenburg, Royal Saxe, and Royal Frankfort[1]. These trade names appear in red or gold block letters, and include "Germany" to denote the country of origin.

At the turn of the twentieth century, there was an increased demand for functional and decorative articles of high quality, made of both glass and china. In 1898, there was an importation of "Royal Vienna" type porcelain vases, painted entirely by hand. Less than a year later, the New York firm of Bawo and Dotter offered "clever imitations", selling at a fraction of the cost. The objects illustrated in the B & D Bulletin, and shown in Appendix 9, were made to order at the Erdmann Schlegelmilch porcelain factory[2]. At this point, Reinhold's firm had not yet switched to large transfers for the decoration of their china. However, this conversion, and the change to colorful backgrounds took place shortly thereafter. By 1902, the colors and transfer subjects used on decorative objects marked with Royal Vienna Germany are found on ordinary R.S. Prussia tableware illustrated in wholesale trade catalogs. Clearly, Reinhold's firm then possessed all the technology needed to make the richly decorated objects which could be substituted for completely hand painted Royal Vienna.

China marked with Royal Vienna Germany (like other trade names discussed in Chapter 3) has not been attributed to Reinhold's firm in recent publications[3]. Although Mary F. Gaston included Royal Vienna with other R.S. Prussia products in Series 4 (Gaston, 1994), it was maintained as a separate section owing to the "unknown" link to Schlegelmilch china. The background for this position, coupled with the potential for a Japanese origin, was discussed in a recent presentation at the annual International Convention of R.S. Prussia Collectors[4]. Two of the reasons cited at the time for the non-Schlegelmilch origin of the Royal Vienna Germany trade name warrant further comment.

First, Royal Vienna Germany was described as a "second level" mark, for it does not incorporate any reference to Reinhold's firm (eg. R.S.), nor is it known to appear in combination with an R.S. trademark. Under these circumstances, and in the absence of other documentation, the mark could have originated with any one of a hundred different contemporary porcelain manufacturers. The absence of a descriptor linking the Royal Vienna Germany trade name to Reinhold's factory has also been noted by R.H. Capers, who attributes this mark to another, but unknown, European decorating firm[5]. In our opinion, the lack of a characteristic to link this mark to Reinhold's firm is not sufficient reason to think Royal Vienna Germany originated elsewhere. Actually, we are surprised **any** of the Royal Vienna Germany molds can be associated with R.S. Prussia. One would **not** expect the firm to have marked these products in any way to detract from their being sold as inexpensive alternates to genuine Royal Vienna[6] imitations. The few objects made from Royal Vienna Germany molds, but marked with RS trademarks, may have resulted from the use of these molds after the trade name had been discontinued.

Second, Gaston suggests an underglaze "beehive" would have been used for a mark on decorative ware if Reinhold's firm intended to profit from the manufacture and sale of Royal Vienna type products. If this were true, then the beehive should also have been used by Erdmann Schlegelmilch for the products sold by Bawo and Dotter. In fact, however, the beehive mark does not appear on this ware. Objects matching the illustration in the B & D Bulletin are marked with "Royal Saxe", Germany, crown, and "E.S."[7]. In our opinion, the use of Royal Vienna Germany by Reinhold's firm simply followed the lead of their major competitor.

In retrospect, we find the real link between Royal Vienna Germany and Reinhold's firm to have been overlooked. In The *Collector's Encyclopedia of R.S. Prussia*, Series 3 (Gaston, 1993), a tall, complex handled ewer made from Mold RVG 17 is illustrated (along with other R.S. products) in pictures from the 1992-93 exhibit of Schlegelmilch china at Suhl, East Germany. The items in this display were owned by local townspeople, including descendants of factory workers, so there is little doubt of their origin. Examples of this ewer in American collections, with identical transfers in either cobalt or peacock blue background colors, are marked with the Royal Vienna Germany trade name.

The origin of other trade names may be traced by the markings on identical objects. For example, the "Lady with Fan" transfer appears on one of the series of four bowls in RS Steeple Mold 9 illustrated in *The Treasures of R.S. Prussia* (Barlock and Barlock, 1976). This example is marked with the classic R.S. Prussia Wreath. The identical bowl is shown in Capers (Capers, 1996), but here it is marked with a red Royal Coburg Germany. We are sure more identities of this type will be found as collectors begin to look for them.

The only area where we lack definitive information about the Royal Vienna Germany trade name concerns the period of use. To date, we have not found examples of Reinhold's decorative objects in pre-1905 trade literature. However, we believe it is possible to establish the earliest possible date of manufacture from the first known use of the decorating transfers. Two of the most frequently used decals on Royal Vienna Germany (red) marked objects are "Diana" and "Flora". These decals begin to appear on R.S. Prussia tableware in the Fall of 1902. Closely following in 1903 are the series of Victorian Vignettes (eg. Lady with Fan), and the "Italian head" series (eg. Litta, Flossie). Other transfers, such as the Artist Portrait series (eg. Recamier), and the "Cottage" series (eg. mill scene), make their debut on tableware manufactured for the 1904 Holiday season.

The overlap of mold and transfer patterns suggests the red and gold versions of the Royal Vienna Germany marks preceded the use of the simpler gold Royal Vienna mark without "Germany" (Capers mark RS 5.3(G) 2). Tableware molds marked with a gold Royal Vienna Germany date from as early as 1901. In contrast, the gold Royal Vienna mark appears on molds known to be made (primarily) after 1905[8]. We know of no case where a Royal Vienna Germany mark appears in conjunction with the classic RS Prussia Wreath. In contrast, the gold Royal Vienna is often found with this mark. The available information leads us to conclude the change from the red (and possibly gold) Royal Vienna Germany to the Royal Vienna (gold, without "Germany") mark was made in 1905, when the firm changed the country of origin in their trademark from Germany to Prussia.

One of the major colors used on Royal Vienna Germany objects decorated with either Flora or Diana the Huntress scenic transfers is described in trade catalogs as "peacock" blue. This luster finish is unusual for two reasons. First, while the blue/green color was clearly intended, parts of some pieces turned out to be plum colored. We think this is due to a partial oxidation during the final color firing. Second, while the gold stencils adhere well and last when applied over peacock blue, they wear excessively when applied to plum colored areas. We have seen plum colored objects with only remnants of the applied gold stencils. Consequently, the extent of conversion to purple and the quality of gold decoration are major factors in the value of Royal Vienna Germany objects with peacock colors.

The illustrations in Chapter 4 are presented differently than other chapters. We continue to record new mold patterns, so we cannot organize them in a logical fashion. We begin with mold patterns known to be decorated with portrait and scenic transfers. Objects marked with a gold Royal Vienna Germany mark conclude Chapter 4. We use and extend the Royal Vienna mold nomenclature developed by Mary F. Gaston (Gaston, 1994). Since no distinction was made between Royal Vienna Germany and Royal Vienna molds, we first extract the Royal Vienna Germany molds, then continue the numbering to include new Royal Vienna Germany patterns.

Endnotes

1. The notation for these marks given in *Capers Notes on the Marks of Prussia* (Alphabet Printing, 1996) are, respectively: RS 5.3R 16; RS 5.3R 17; RS 5.3R 20; not shown; and RS 5.3R 5.

2. Objects in these shapes are also shown by Mary F. Gaston in Series 1 (Gaston 1986) and by R. H. Capers (Capers, 1996).

3. For the discussion in support of Royal Vienna originating from an outside decorating studio, see p. 168 in Series 4 (Gaston, 1995), and p. 69 of *Capers Notes* (Alphabet Printing, 1996).

4. The origin of Royal Vienna Germany was the feature presentation at the 12th annual convention of the Int'l Assoc. of R.S. Prussia Collectors, Inc.

5. Capers suggests objects made from undocumented Royal Vienna Germany molds may have been obtained as "white blanks" from other porcelain manufacturers. However, this explanation cannot apply to many of the marked examples. Cobalt blue is a common background color for this ware, and it is not applied to glazed ware, or "white blanks" as suggested. Cobalt blue must be applied to the clay blank at the low fired (or glowpaste) stage of manufacture. Then, after the application of the glaze components, a special high temperature "sharp" firing generates the characteristic blue color. Normally, cobalt bleeds into the glaze, producing a diffuse boundary between painted and unpainted sections. On better decorated items, the fuzzy margins are covered with a narrow band of gold.

6. It does not appear the manufacture of Royal Vienna Germany products was an attempt to deceive American customers. The products made under this trade name are neither counterfeits or reproductions, and are best described as imitations.

7. The Capers (Capers, 1996) notation for this mark is ES 3.4G 2. The mark is also shown in Appendix 9.

8. The gold Royal Vienna mark may also be found on earlier molds kept in production past 1905, such as RSP Mold 256.

Plate 604. Vase, red/green, Royal Vienna Germany (RVG) Mold 1, Potocka portrait decor, 10.5" h. Mirror image shape to RV Mold 1. Marked Royal Vienna Germany (red). $900-$1300.

Plate 607. Vase, sunset colors, RVG Mold 2, Cottage scenic decor, 7.37" h. Marked Royal Vienna Germany (red). $600-$900.

Plate 605. Vase, cobalt, RVG Mold 2 (also RSP Mold 944), Lady Watering Flowers scenic decor, 7.37" h. Marked Royal Vienna Germany (red). $900-$1300.

Plate 606. Vase, bronze/gold Moire, RVG Mold 2, Lady with Fan scenic decor, 7.37" h. Marked Royal Vienna Germany (red). $900-$1300.

Plate 609. Vase, red/green, RVG Mold 2, LeBrun portrait decor, 6" h. Marked Royal Vienna Germany (gold). $900-$1300.

Plate 608. Vase, yellow top, RVG Mold 2, Cottage scenic decor, 6.5" h. Unmarked. $400-$600.

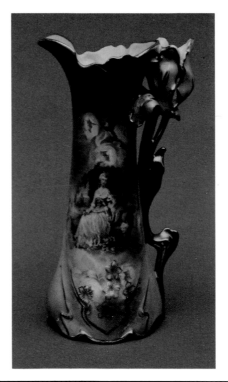

Plate 611. Iris handled ewer, yellow/purple/blue, RVG Mold 5, Lady with Dog scenic decor, 7" h. Unmarked. $900-$1300.

Plate 610. Ewer, satin bronze gold RVG Mold 3, Diana the Huntress scenic decor, 8.5" h. Marked Royal Vienna Germany (red). $2500+

Plate 612. Iris handled ewer, peacock blue, RVG Mold 5, Lady Feeding Chickens scenic decor, 12" h. Marked Royal Vienna Germany (red). $2500+

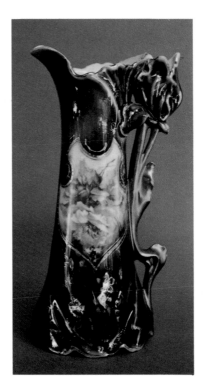

Plate 613. Iris handled ewer, cobalt, RVG Mold 5, orange rose decor, 6.75" h. Marked Royal Vienna Germany (red). $600-$900.

Plate 614. Iris handled ewer, reverse of Plate 612, RVG Mold 5, Lady Watering Flowers scenic decor.

Plate 615. Iris handled ewer, red/green, RVG Mold 5, LeBrun portrait decor, 10" h. Marked Royal Vienna (gold). $2500++

Plate 618. Two handled vase, peacock blue, RVG Mold 7, white band with Diana the Huntress decor, 10.25" h. Marked Royal Vienna Germany (red). $600-$900.

Plate 616. Iris handled ewer, yellow top, RVG Mold 5, pansy decor, 8.75" h. Marked Royal Vienna Germany (red). $900-$1300.

Plate 617. Iris handled ewer, peacock colors, RVG Mold 5, pink rose decor, 7" h. Marked Royal Vienna Germany (red). $900-$1300.

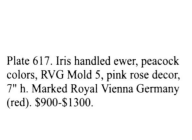

Plate 619. Two handled vase, yellow/ green, RVG Mold 7, decor HI 3, 7" h. Marked Royal Vienna Germany (red). $75-$100.

Plate 622. Two handled vase, peacock blue, RV Mold 12, pink rose decor, 8.75" h. Marked Royal Vienna Germany (red). $400-$600.

Plate 620. Two handled vase, cobalt, RVG Mold 12 mirror image to RV 12, Tillie portrait decor, 4.25" h. Marked Royal Vienna Germany (red). $400-$600.

Plate 624. Two handled vase, red/green, RV Mold 13, Potocka portrait decor, 9" h. Marked Royal Vienna Germany (gold). $900-$1300.

Plate 621. Two handled vase, yellow/green, RV Mold 12, Cottage scenic decor, 4.5" h. $250-$400.

Plate 623. Two handled vase, yellow/green, RV Mold 12, Castle scenic decor, 8.37" h. Marked Royal Vienna Germany (red). $400-$600.

Plate 625. Ewer, deep blue, RVG Mold 16, decor HI, 10.75" h. Marked Saxe Altenburg Germany. $250-$400.

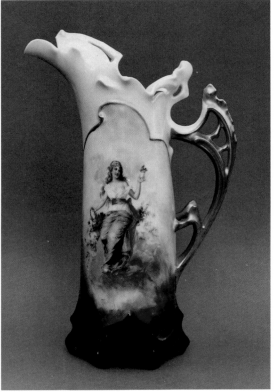

Plate 627. Tankard, RVG Mold 17 (also RSP Mold 640), yellow top, Lady with Bird Allegorical scene decor, 12" h. Rare. $2500.

Plate 628. Tankard, cobalt, RVG Mold 17, Flora scenic decor, 12" h. $2500++

Plate 626. Ewer, peacock blue, RVG Mold 16, Diana the Huntress scenic decor, 11" h. Marked Royal Vienna Germany (red). $600-$900.

Plate 629. Tankard, peacock blue, RVG Mold 17, Cherubs decor, 6" h. Marked Royal Vienna Germany (red). $400-$600.

Plate 632. Tankard, green, RVG Mold 17, Woman in Red portrait decor, 5" h. Marked Saxe Altenburg Germany. $250-$400.

Plate 630. Tankard, reverse side of Plate 628, Diana the Huntress scenic decor.

Plate 633. Ewer, peacock blue, RVG Mold 18 (also RSP Mold 959), Diana the Huntress scenic decor, 7.75" h. Marked Royal Vienna Germany (red). $900-$1300.

Plate 631. Tankard, reverse side of Plate 629, RVG Mold 17, cherubs (different) decor.

Plate 634. Ewer, green, RVG Mold 18, decor HI 3, 4.75" h. Marked Royal Vienna Germany (red). $100-$150.

Plate 635. Ewer, green, RVG Mold 18, orange rose decor, 7.75" h. Marked Royal Vienna Germany (red). $250-$400.

Plate 638. Vase, plum, RVG Mold 19, Diana the Huntress scenic decor, 8.5" h. Marked Royal Vienna Germany (red). $250-$400.

Plate 636. Ewer, red/green, RVG Mold 18, LeBrun portrait decor, 8.5" h. Marked Royal Vienna Germany (gold). $1300-$1800.

Plate 639. Vase, satin red shading to peacock blue, RVG Mold 19, 7.25" h. Very scarce red coloration. Marked Royal Vienna Germany (red). $150-$250.

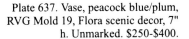

Plate 637. Vase, peacock blue/plum, RVG Mold 19, Flora scenic decor, 7" h. Unmarked. $250-$400.

Plate 640. Vase, peacock blue, RVG
Mold 20, Diana the Huntress scenic
decor with cupids series 1, 8.75" h.
Unmarked. $400-$600.

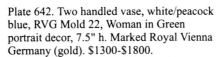

Plate 642. Two handled vase, white/peacock
blue, RVG Mold 22, Woman in Green
portrait decor, 7.5" h. Marked Royal Vienna
Germany (gold). $1300-$1800.

Plate 643. Vase, peacock blue, RVG Mold
23, Lady Watering Flowers scenic decor, 9"
h. Marked Royal Vienna Germany (red).
$900-$1300.

Plate 641. Two handled vase, purple/blue, RVG Mold
22 (also RSP Mold 945), Lady Feeding Chickens
scenic decor, 6" h. Royal Vienna Germany (red).
$1300-$1800.

Plate 644. Two handled vase, purple/yellow,
RVG Mold 26, pansy decor, 7.25" h.
Marked Royal Vienna Germany (red). $250-
$400.

Plate 645. Ewer, peacock blue, RVG Mold 28, cherubs decor, 4" h. Marked Royal Vienna Germany (red). $250-$400.

Plate 647. Ewer, purple/yellow, RVG Mold 28, pansy decor, 7.25" h. Marked Royal Vienna Germany (red). $150-$250.

Plate 648. Ewer, peacock blue, RVG Mold 28, Flora scenic decor, 9" h. Marked Royal Vienna Germany (red). $900-$1300.

Plate 646. Ewer, bronze/peacock blue, RVG Mold 28, pink flower decor, 6" h. Marked Royal Vienna Germany (red). $250-$400.

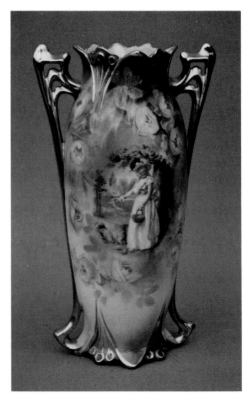

Plate 649. Two handled vase, purple/yellow, RVG Mold 30, Lady Feeding Chickens scenic decor, 7" h. Marked Royal Vienna Germany (red). $1800-$2300.

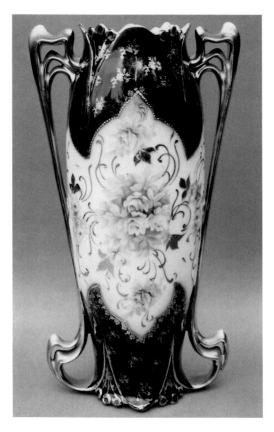

Plate 650. Two handled vase, cobalt, RVG Mold 30, pink floral decor, 14.25" h. Marked Royal Coburg Germany. $1300-$1800.

Plate 653. Two handled vase, peacock blue, RVG Mold 34 (similar to RV Mold 11), Flora scenic decor, 8.75" h. Marked Royal Vienna Germany (red). $600-$900.

Plate 651. Two handled vase, browns, RVG Mold 30, Flossie portrait decor, 7" h. Marked Royal Vienna Germany (red). $400-$600.

Plate 652. Pedestal shaped two handled vase, cobalt, RVG Mold 32, Potocka portrait decor, 8.75" h. Marked Royal Vienna Germany (red). $1300-$1800.

Plate 654. Two handled vase, bronze, RVG Mold 34, pink rose decor, 7.5" h. Marked Royal Vienna Germany (red). $250-$400.

147

Plate 655. Two handled vase, cobalt, RVG Mold 36, Potocka portrait decor, 10.25" h. Marked Royal Vienna Germany (gold). $1300-$1800.

Plate 658. Two handled vase, peacock blue at top, RVG Mold 40, LeBrun portrait decor, 9" h. Royal Vienna Germany (gold). $1300-$1800.

Plate 656. Vase with side ornaments, RVG Mold 37, LeBrun portrait decor, 9.75" h. Marked Royal Vienna Germany (gold). $1300-$1800.

Plate 657. Two handled vase, browns, RVG Mold 40, Tillie portrait decor, 5" h. Marked Royal Coburg Germany (red). $150-$250.

Below: Plate 659. Two handled vase, cobalt, RVG Mold 40, Lady Watering Flowers scenic decor, 7.12" h. Marked Royal Vienna Germany (red). $1300-$1800.

Plate 660. Two handled vase, shaded rose, RVG Mold 40, scarce "Washington" souvenir decor with pink roses, 4.25" h. Marked Royal Vienna Germany (red). $250-$400.

Plate 663. Vase with side ornaments, dark blue, RVG Mold 43, decor HI 2, 9.75" h. Marked Royal Vienna Germany (red). $250-$400.

Plate 662. Bottle vase, plum/peacock blue, RVG Mold 41, Flora scenic decor, 8.5" h. Marked Royal Vienna Germany (red). $400-$600

Plate 661. Two handled vase, yellow/green, RVG Mold 40, Cottage scenic decor, 5" h. Marked Royal Vienna Germany (red). $250-$400.

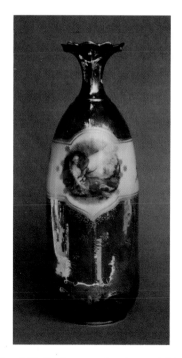

Plate 664. Bottle vase, plum/peacock blue, RVG Mold 45, Diana the Huntress scenic decor, 9" h. Marked Royal Vienna Germany (red). $400-$600.

Plate 665. Vase with leaf top, yellow/ green, RVG Mold 47, Mill scenic decor, 9.5" h. Marked Royal Vienna Germany (red). $900-$1300.

Plate 668. Two handled vase, green tint, RVG Mold 48, pink floral decor, 8.75" h. Marked Royal Vienna Germany (red). $600-$900.

Plate 667. Vase with leaf top, green tint, RVG Mold 47, pink floral decor, 9.5" h. Marked Royal Vienna Germany (red). $900-$1300.

Plate 666. Vase with leaf top, sunset colors, RVG Mold 47, Castle scenic decor, 9.5" h. Marked Royal Vienna Germany (red). $900-$1300.

Plate 669. Vase with side ornaments, red browns, RVG Mold 50, decor HI 2, 7" h. $150-$250.

Plate 670. Vase with side ornaments, cobalt, RVG Mold 51, Lady with Fan scenic decor, 7" h. $900-$1300.

Plate 672. Vase with side ornaments, red/green, RVG Mold 53, Potocka portrait decor, 7" h. Marked Royal Vienna Germany (gold). $400-$600.

Plate 673. Vase, cobalt, RVG Mold 55, Lady Feeding Chickens scenic decor, 7.12" h. Unmarked. $600-$900.

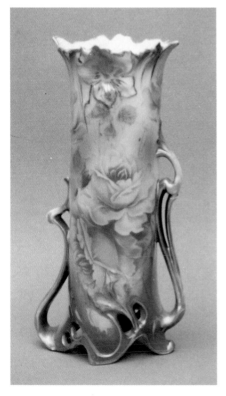

Plate 671. Vase with side ornaments, yellow/pink, RVG Mold 51, red rose decor, 6.62" h. Marked Royal Vienna Germany (gold). $150-$250.

Plate 674. Two handled vase, yellow/pink, RVG Mold 58, pink rose decor, 11.25" h. Marked Royal Vienna Germany (gold). $600-$900.

Plate 675. Two handled vase, plum/peacock blue, RVG Mold 60 (also RSP Mold 943), Potocka portrait decor, Unmarked, 11" h. $2500+

Plate 678. Covered, handled urn, plum/peacock blue, RVG Mold 62, Flora scenic decor, 11.25" h. Royal Vienna Germany (red). $1300-$1800.

Plate 677. Covered, handled urn, peacock blue, RVG Mold 62, pink roses decor, 11.25" h. Marked Royal Vienna Germany (red). $900-$1300.

Plate 676. Two handled vase, blue/yellow, RVG Mold 60, pink roses decor, 11" h. Marked Royal Vienna Germany (gold). $400-$600.

Plate 679. Two handled vase, green, RVG Mold 64, decor HI 2, 11" h. Unmarked. $250-$400.

Plate 680. Pedestal vase with side ornaments, cobalt, RVG Mold 65, Potocka portrait decor, 7.75" h. Marked Royal Vienna Germany (gold). $600-$900.

Plate 683. Vase with side ornaments, RVG Mold 69, Recamier portrait decor, 9" h. Marked Royal Saxe Germany. $600-$900.

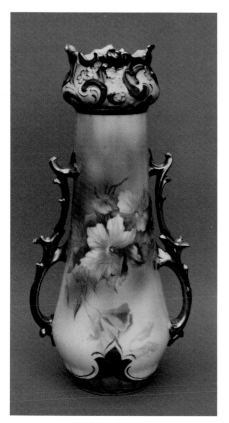

Plate 682. Vase with side ornaments, yellow/green, RVG Mold 68, LeBrun portrait decor, 9" h. Marked Royal Saxe Germany. $600-$900.

Plate 681. Vase with side oraments, purple/yellow, RVG Mold 68, clematis decor, 11.62" h. Marked Royal Vienna Germany (gold). $400-$600.

Plate 684. Bottle vase, yellow/green, RVG Mold 71, Potocka portrait decor, 5.5" h. Marked Royal Vienna Germany (gold). $400-$600.

Plate 687. Vase, red/green, RVG Mold 75 (also RSP Mold 907), Potocka portrait decor, 4.75" h. Marked Royal Vienna Germany (gold). $400-$600.

Plate 685. Bottle vase, peacock blue/white, RVG Mold 71, LeBrun portrait decor, 4.62" h. Marked Royal Vienna Germany (gold). $250-$400.

Plate 688. Pedestal shape handled vase, red/green, RVG Mold 76, Recamier portrait decor, 5" h. Marked Royal Vienna Germany (gold). $600-$900.

Plate 686. Bottle vase, red/green, RVG Mold 73 (also RSP Mold 915), LeBrun portrait decor, 8" h. Marked Royal Vienna Germany (gold). $250-$400.

Plate 689. Bottle vase, red/ green, RSP Mold 910, Potocka portrait decor, 4.5" h. Marked Royal Vienna Germany (gold). $250-$400.

154

Plate 692. Cake plate, red/green, RS Steeple Mold 3, LeBrun portrait decor, 9.5" d. Marked Royal Vienna Germany (gold). $900-$1300.

Plate 690. Bottle vase, red/green, RSP Mold 910, LeBrun portrait decor, 5" h. Marked Royal Vienna Germany (gold). $250-$400.

Plate 691. Cake plate, red/green, RS Steeple Mold 3, Potocka portrait decor, 9.5" d. Marked Royal Vienna Germany (gold). $900-$1300.

Plate 693. Salad bowl, red/chocolate brown, RSP Mold 98, Potocka portrait decor, 10" d. Marked Royal Vienna Germany (gold). $900-$1300.

Plate 694. Cake plate, red/chocolate brown, RSP Mold 98, Recamier portrait decor, 10.75" d. Marked Royal Vienna Germany (gold). $900-$1300.

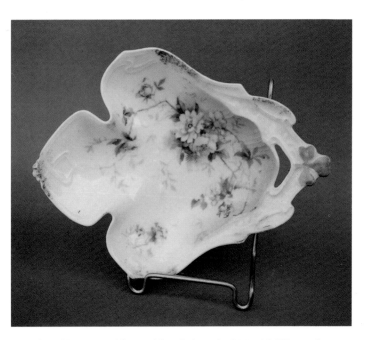

Plate 695. Tray, white, mold variation of RSP Mold 802, small rose decor. Marked Royal Vienna Germany (gold). $75-$100.

Plate 697. Plate, white rim, RS Steeple Mold 3, pink floral decor, 9" d. Marked Royal Vienna Germany (gold). $150-$250.

Plate 696. Salad bowl, peacock blue/white, RVG 102, decor HI 5, 11.25" d. The identical bowl was offered as R2298 with metallic luster finish by Butler Bros. in a late 1903 catalog. Marked Royal Vienna Germany (gold). $150-$250.

Plate 698. Plate, red rim, RS Steeple Mold 3, pink floral decor, 9" d. Marked Royal Vienna Germany (gold). $150-$250.

Plate 699. Heart shape salad bowl, white/buff edge, decor HI 4, 10" d. Marked Royal Vienna Germany (gold). $250-$400.

Plate 700. Chocolate pot, purple top, RSP Mold 502, dropped rose decor, 9" h. Marked Royal Vienna Germany (gold). $250-$400.

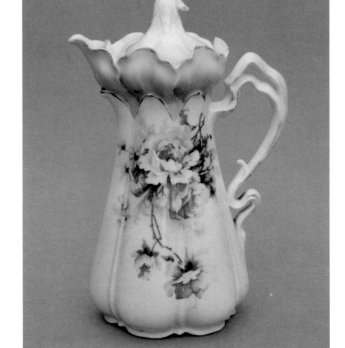

References

Barlock, George and Barlock, Eileen. *The Treasures of R.S. Prussia*. Parkersburg WV: Pappas Bros., 1976

Capers, R.H. *Capers Notes on the Marks of Prussia*, El Paso, IL: Alphabet Printing, 1996

Gaston, M.F. The *Collector's Encyclopedia of R.S. Prussia*, First Series. Paducah, KY: Collector Books, 1982

Gaston, M.F. The *Collector's Encyclopedia of R.S. Prussia*, Second Series. Paducah, KY: Collector Books, 1986

Gaston, M.F. The *Collector's Encyclopedia of R.S. Prussia*, Third Series. Paducah, KY: Collector Books, 1994

Gaston, M.F. *Collector's Encyclopedia of R.S. Prussia*, Fourth Series. Paducah, KY: Collector Books, 1994

Lechler, Doris A., *French and German Dolls, Dishes and Accessories*, Marietta, OH: Antique Publications, 1991

Terrell, George W. Jr. *Collecting R.S. Prussia*. Florence, AL: Books Americana, 1982

Appendix 1
Update on Early R.S. Prussia Mold Patterns

Information about the early porcelain china produced by Reinhold Schlegelmilch continues to be developed by interested collectors. Here, we provide an update on recent discoveries. Foremost, we have acquired more examples of the "A" series of molds, including a marked example. It was also brought to our attention that Mold A3 is shown in the 1894-1896 Butler Bros. catalogs. This provides a greater confidence in their R.S. origin, and has allowed us to identify still other molds to have been made by the firm.

We have learned of more examples of marked objects in OM mold patterns not known to be marked at the time of preparation of the first book. An RS Wing marked example of the Scallop Bottom Mold, OM 130, has been found. The mark is consistent with the illustration of this pattern in the 1898 Webb-Freyschlag catalog. A cup/saucer set in Mold OM 152 has been found with the classic RS Prussia Wreath. This mark is consistent with the longer lifetime of toys, mugs, and cup/saucer sets.

No examples of "RS Arrow" marked objects have decoration matching any pattern used on objects in our updated mold pattern-transfer outline matrix. While some "raised dot" decorations on these objects are similar to those on the series of A molds, we have yet to find an identity to extend our mold/transfer matrix to RS Arrow marked objects.

Plate 701. Cake plate, peach rim, Mold A2 variation, blue flower decor, 10.25"d. $50-$75.

Plate 702. Cake plate, orange rim, Mold A2 variation, orange flower decals, 10.25" d. $50-$75.

Plate 703. Cake plate, white, Mold A3, cascade of orange flowers, 11.25" d. $50-$75.

Plate 704. Cake plate, Mold A3, brown behind thistle type leaves, 11.25" d. $50-$75.

Plate 705. Cake plate, white with applied dots, Mold A 6, pink floral center, 11" d. $100-$200.

Plate 706. Cake plate, dusty rose edge, white with applied dots, Mold A 6, leaf decor, 11" d. $100-$200.

Plate 706A. Example of the Made in Germany mark found on a cake plate in Mold A3, and on other very early R.S. Prussia examples. Also used in combination with "U.S. Pat.". While a patent may have been applied for, one was never issued in the United States.

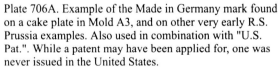

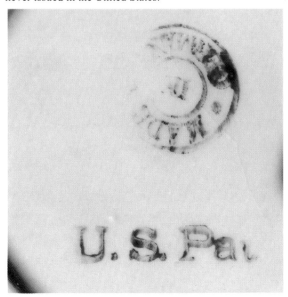

Plate 707. Cake plate, white edge, Mold A 6, strawberries on blue background, 11" d. $75-$100.

Appendix 2
Cupid and Scenic Vignette Transfers

Beginning in 1902, a short series of six Allegorical scenes were used on R.S. Prussia tableware illustrated in wholesale trade catalogs. Usually, these transfers were quite small, and are found mainly in the reserves of rims. Two other series of courting scenes were used, both for reserves and as the central decoration. These transfers were used on unmarked R.S. Prussia molds, and are not shown in other reference books on R.S. Prussia.

A long series of cupid scenes was used in reserves, often in combination with large transfers of Flora or Diana the Huntress.

We suspect there are more cupid scenes than are illustrated here. This long series was used on objects made from RSP Mold 343, Molds RS 34 and RS 36, as well as many Royal Vienna Germany molds. A shorter series of cupid scenes was used in the reserves of objects made in mold RS 6. The overall appearance of these transfers is quite different from those used on other R.S. Prussia molds.

Plate 708. Detail of Allegorical scenes used on R.S. Prussia

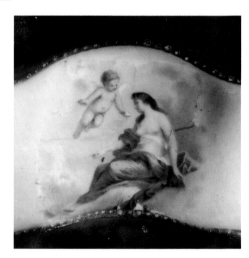

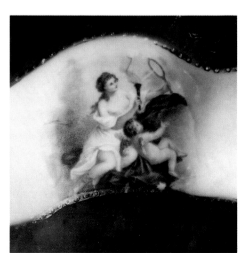

Plate 709. Detail of Cupid series 1 transfers used on R.S. Prussia

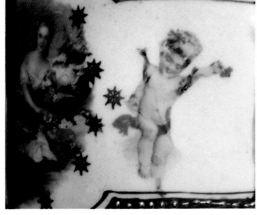

Plate 710. Detail of Cupid Series 2 transfers used on R.S. Prussia

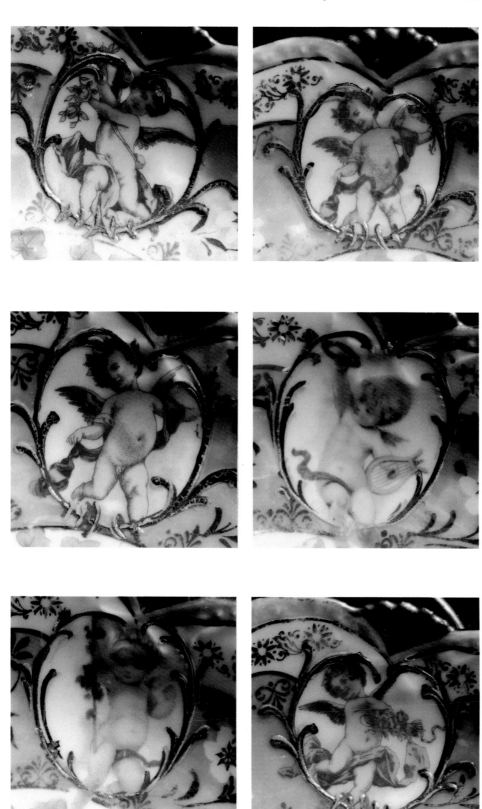

Plate 711. Detail of Colonial transfers.

Appendix 3
Mineral Transfers from
C.A. Pocher, G.M.B.H.

A sales catalog of mineral transfers (decals) from the German firm of C.A. Pocher, G.M.B.H., is in the collection of the Strong Museum Library at Rochester, New York. These decals were attached to pages, along with a sticker showing order number, quantity per sheet, and price (in Reichmarks). Although there is no recorded date, this appears to be a collection put together between 1900 and 1915, based on the subject matter of the transfers. Cumulative sales brochures or catalogs were an easy way to display what a manufacturing firm could offer. In addition to the portrait series shown here, many other transfer types in this collection were used on R.S. Prussia. They include "The Cage" (both mirror image forms), the "Dice Throwers" and "Melon Boys", the "Nightwatch", and the two Nymphs (on rock, pouring water) also shown in *Encyclopedia of R.S. Prussia*, Series 2, Plates 533-534.

Plate 712. Page in the C.S. Pocher catalog showing the Artist series of mineral transfers. This firm also carried many other transfers used on R.S. Prussia. *Courtesy of the Strong Museum Library.*

Appendix 4
Update on R.S. Prussia Toy Tea Sets

Many Art Nouveau shaped toy tea sets are illustrated by Doris A. Lechler in *French and German Dolls, Dishes, and Accessories*, (Antique Publications, Marietta, OH, 1991). Most of the information for the time of manufacture for R.S. Prussia sets can now be updated. For the set in each Figure listed below, we provide the estimated time of manufacture of the set (as reported), and our revised range of dates based on trade catalog illustrations of the mold pattern, and the known periods of transfer use.

Figure	Cited Year(s)	Revised Year(s)
299	Late 19th century	1903-1905
300	1880-1900	1904-1908
301	1885-1900	1904-1908
302	Late 19th century	1904-1908
303	1890-1900	1904-1908
304	ca.1920	1904-1908
305	1890-1920	Hybrid set[1], 1905 (cream/sugar)
306	Turn of century	1905-1911[2]
307	Turn of century	1903-1911
308-9	Early 20th century	Hybrid set[3], 1905-1910
310	1890-1900	1905-1910
311	1900-1920	1898-1905
313	1890-1900	1908-1910
314	1880-1900	1905-1910
315	1900-1915	Hybrid set[4] 1898-1905
316	ca. 1900	1898-1905
317	1900-1915	1898-1905
318	1920	1905-1910[5]
319	1915-1920	1903-1910
321	1915	1903-1910
322	1915	1905-1910
323	1915	1905-1910
324	1920	1898-1904
325	1915-1925	Tableware pattern[6] 1904-1906
326	1915-1925	1905-1912
331	Turn of century	1898-1907[7]
332	1870-1885	Part of tête-à-tête set[8], 1901-1904
333	*	1905-1910
335	*	1906-1910
337	1900-1920	1905-1908
339	1900-1920	1903-1905
351	1890-1930	1896-1900
379	Turn of century	1911

Several R.S. Prussia toy sets are shown by Lorraine Punchard in *Playtime Pottery and Porcelain* (Schiffer Publ., 1996). The sets decorated with printed transfers were made after 1900. Revised dates of manufacture for these sets are listed below by page number and position.

Page/ place	Cited Year(s)	Revised Year(s)
p. 37T	1890-1914[9]	1896-1900
p. 37M	nd	1896-1900[10]
p. 39M	1880-1890[11]	1896-1900
p. 39B	1880-1890	1896-1900
p. 70	1869-1910[12]	1906-1908
p. 71/T	early 1900s[13]	1901-1905
p. 71/B	1869-1910	1909-1911
p. 72/T	1869-1910	1908[14]
p. 72/M	1869-1910	1906-1910
p. 72/B	1869-1910	1910-1914
p. 73/T	1869-1910	1905[15]
p. 73/M	1869-1910	1901-1904[16]
p. 116/Bl		1900-1904[17]

Webb-Freyschlag was an important distributor of R.S. Prussia during 1900-1903, and possibly beyond. Their Fall catalog for 1903 shows a large selection of china toy tea sets broken down into two sections, each corresponding to a different inventory code. Their line of "PERFECTION" toy tea sets is described as "A high grade line of child's toy sets, a better class of goods than other jobbers bring to this country and at the same prices they ask for inferior goods." We reproduce here this entire section showing several tea sets in known R.S. Prussia mold patterns. Note the lids of tea pots in less expensive sets generally overhang, while the lids of the higher priced sets rest inside the pot. While we cannot be absolutely sure, we suspect this entire line was made by Reinhold Schlegelmilch.

Endnotes

1. Teapot and cup/saucer not same mold as cream/sugar (a tableware mold), as originally sold.

2. Toy chocolate sets are not shown in any of the numerous wholesale trade catalogs we have examined dating from 1890 through 1916. In the absence of matching plates and/or shipping box, we suspect this is a combination of a tall syrup can and after dinner cup/saucers. Both of these items were sold separately, but could be ordered with the same decoration. Items marked with the classic R.S. Prussia Wreath (red mark) were made between 1905 and 1910.

3. Cup/saucer sets are not the same mold as cream/sugar and teapot, and they are the size of demitasse cup/saucers. Most toy tea sets in this pattern were sold with this combination of sizes and molds, but cup/saucer sets in a mold matching the teapot were made. This pattern first appears in 1905.

4. Teapot mold does not match rest of set, as originally sold.

5. This decoration only appears on mold patterns marked with the classic RS Prussia Wreath.

6. This is another example of a toy tea set in a tableware pattern. The tableware sold (primarily) between 1904 and 1906.

7. A tea set (partial) in this mold (shown decorated with roses and snowballs) is illustrated in Plate 606 of *R.S. Prussia - The Early Years* (Schiffer Publ., 1997). This mold is illustrated in a Fall/Winter 1898 Eisinger, Kramer and Co. wholesale catalog. Examples are also known to be decorated with Hidden Image transfers.

8. The Morning Glory pattern (RSP Mold 502) was used for tableware from 1901 to 1904.

9. The origin of this set is Germany, not France. One characteristic of early German toy tea sets is the gold line painting on the front of the teapot spout. In addition, the molds used for the lids were often changed (cf. set on p. 39).

10. The mold pattern for this set is the same as in Plate 606 in *R.S. Prussia - The Early Years*.

11. The marking on the box "DEPONIRT, S&T" translates to "Export (product), Suhl and Tillowitz".

12. This R.S. Prussia mold was sold as a combination dinner and tea set, containing a tea pot, cream/sugar, 6 cup/saucers, 6 plates, and 2 perforated trays (not shown). Catalog descriptions of these oversize sets include their use for after dinner coffees.

13. A set with provenance.

14. This "finest quality R.S. china" set was offered by G. Sommers & Co. in their Fall 1908 catalog.

15. This set was offered by Butler Bros. in their Fall 1905 catalog.

16. This is an early mold, OM 13, first used for tableware in 1898, but the transfer on this set was not used on tableware until 1901.

17. This is not a toy chocolate, but a full size pot sold for a few years after 1900 (Mold OM 150). The heights of regulation size chocolate pots during 1900-1903 range from 5.5" to 11.5". Below this size, similar shapes are described as tall syrup cans.

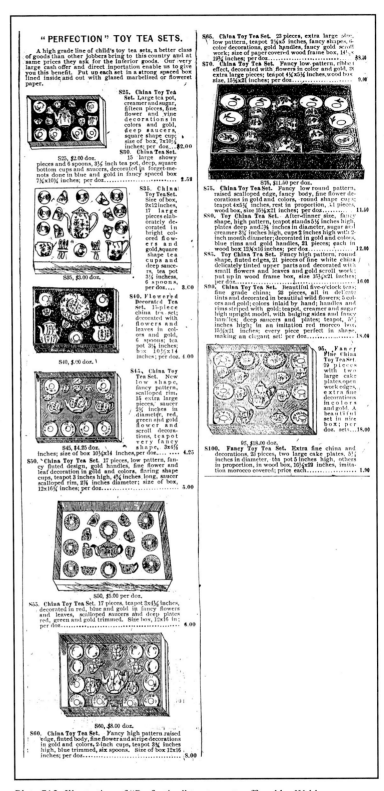

Plate 713. Illustration of "Perfection" toy tea sets offered by Webb-Freyschlag in the Sept. 1903 catalog. In this collection, S35, S40, S45, and S60 are products from Reinhold Schlegelmilch. *Courtesy of Amador Collections, Rio Grande Historical Collection, State University of New Mexico.*

Appendix 5
Tableware Objects in the Hidden Image Pattern

Over the years, we have kept track of different objects made in the Hidden Image pattern. The list started with about 20 items, and has steadily lengthened. At the beginning of 1997, we thought we had finally achieved a complete listing, as no new objects had been recorded for over a year. However, a new tray and a new bowl appeared at the 1997 International R.S. Prussia Collectors annual convention. Consequently, although comprehensive, the following list is still incomplete. Items in **italics** are those we have not been able to document fully. Collectors having undocumented items and/or items not on this list are encouraged to write us in care of the Publisher.

Number	Item	Size
1	Berry Bowl, Master	10"[1]
2	Berry Bowl, Individual	5"
3	Biscuit Jar,	7.5" h.
4	Bowl, double image	10.5"
5	Bowl, single image	10"
6	Bowl, single image	9"
7	Bowl, single image	7.75"
8	Bowl, single image with raised arm	8.25"
9	Bowl, single image	6.25"
10	Box, stamp (?)	2" x 3"
11	Box, match[2]	2.5" x 5"
12	Box, pin	2.5" x 5"
13	Box, hairpin[3]	2.5" x 5"
14	Box,	3" x 5.5"
15	Box, powder	4" x 5"
16	Box, "	4.5" x 6.5"
17	Box, "	4" x 6.25"
18	Box, hair receiver[4]	4" x 4.75"
19	*Broom holder[5]*	
20	Cake plate, three images	13"
21	Cake plate, double image	11.5"
22	Cake plate, single image	10.5"
23	Cake plate, single image	9.5"
24	Celery tray	12" x 4.5"
25	Chamberstick	3.25" x 6"
26	Chocolate pot	9" h.
27	Chocolate cup/saucer	2.75" h.
28	Coffee cup	2.5" h.
29	Creamer	3.5" h.
30	Creamer, Matches #40	3.5" - 4" h.
31	*Demitasse cup[5]*	
32	Mustache cup	3.5" x 2.5" h.
33	Mustard pot	3.25" h.
34	Mug, plain	3.5" h.
35	Mug, shaving (no mirror)	3.5" h.
36	Pitcher, indiv. milk	4.75" h. x 3.75" d.
37	Pitcher, small (mush set?)	4.75" h. x 3.25" d.
38	Pitcher, milk	6.25" h.
39	Pitcher, cider	7.5" h.
40	Pitcher, water	9" h.
41	Plate, plain	8.5"
42	Plate, plain	7.5 "
43	Plate, plain	5"
44	Relish tray	8.75" x 3.5"
45	Sugar bowl/lid,	4" h.
46	Syrup, with underplate (no profile)	4.5" h.
47	Toothpick holder	2.37" h.
48	Tray, pin	5.25" x 7"
49	Tray, pin	4.5" x 5.5"
50	Tray, pin -torso form on left	6.25"x 4.5"
51	Tray, pin - full face	6" x 4.75"
52	Tray, -torso form on right	4.75" x 6.5"
53	Tray, image on left side	6" x 7"
54	Tray, serving	6.5" x 10.5"
55	Tray, dresser (two profiles)	11" x 7.12"
56	*Tray, bread (2 or 3 images ?)*	*approx. 13" x 9"*
57	Tray, crumb, with brush[5]	
58	Tray, pin (profile in center)	4" x 6"
59	Bowl, beaded edge	11.75" x 10"
60	*Charger (4 images)*	*19"*
61	*Plate, 3 cameo (1 FF, 2 PF)[5]*	
62	Teapot	5.5" x 7.5"
63	*Bowl, very large, four images[5]*	

Endnotes

1. May be same size as #5 or #6.
2. Striker underneath lid.
3. Hairpin embossed on lid.
4. Heart shaped.
5. No dimensions given.

Appendix 6
Examples of Trade Names Used on R.S. Prussia

Just prior to 1900, the Reinhold Schlegelmilch firm began to use trade names as well as trademarks on china for American export. One of the first examples was "Royal Coburg Germany", used on china products illustrated in *The Early Years*. Here, we illustrate trade name marks we are certain to have been used on R.S. Prussia manufactured after 1900. We have cited reasons for the R.S. origin of many of these marks in Chapters 3 and 4. As explained in Chapter 3, the purpose of these marks was to facilitate the sale of the same product to different American distributors.

Plate 714. Detail of marks used on trade named R.S. Prussia.

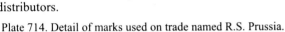

Appendix 7
Sample China Offered by C.E. Wheelock & Co.

The back page color advertisement on the 1903 C.E. Wheelock catalog details the shipment of sample goods to their wholesale firm, and what they did differently in 1903 compared to previous years. R.S. Prussia patterns, identified from other sources, include Nos. 2, 5, 10, 11, 17, 19, 33, and 46. Reproduced with permission from the Amador Collections, Rio Grande Historical Collections, University of New Mexico Library (Las Cruces).

Plate 715. Reprint of back page of the C.E. Wheelock & Co. Fall 1903 catalog showing sample merchandise from European manufacturers. *Courtesy of Amador Collections, Rio Grande Historical Collection, State University of New Mexico.*

Appendix 8
Marks and Corresponding Transfers on Mold #343

RSP Mold 343[1] was heavily used in a short four to five year period. It is one of about a dozen molds used for trade name merchandise. We list here all of the decorations known to be used on this mold, according to trade name or trademark. This listing shows the extent of overlap of a given decoration on both trade name and RS trademarked objects.

Mark	Decoration
Classic RS Prussia Wreath	Season scenics (fall, summer, etc)
	Flora, Diana
	Cupids
Classic RS Wreath[2]	Melon eaters (Miro paintings)
	Roman Women[3]
RS Steeple Prussia (green)	FD J[4]
RS Steeple Germany (red)[5]	FD C (2 white,1 yellow flower)
	FD J
	FD N (3 small pink roses)
	FD U (red + orange roses)
	HI-5 (FD Q-pink, white, yellow mums)
	HI-5 (bent yellow rose)[6]
Royal Vienna + crown (gold)[7]	Not numbered, azaleas and lilies
Viersa + crown[8]	FD N
	FD S (3 yellow roses)
	HI-13 (Saxe FDb-1[9],3 small flowers)
	HI-12 (Saxe FDb-2, 3 red/pink roses)
Saxe Altenburg Germany[10]	FD U
	HI-1 (FD R)
	HI-5 (FD Q)
	Star FDa (2 buds+large aster)
	Saxe FDa (azaleas)
	Saxe FDd (daffodils)
	HI-14 (stylized flowers)
	Mythological figures[11]

Mark	Decoration
Saxe Altenburg Germany + crown[12]	HI-5 (FD Q)
	HI-13 (Saxe FDb-1)
Royal Coburg Germany[13]	HI-5 (FD Q)
	Star FDa
	Star FDb (phlox)
	Star FDc (2 red,1 yellow mum)
	HI-13 (Saxe FDb-1)
	Saxe FDd
	Victorian scenes[14]
Royal Frankfort Germany[15]	HI-14 (stylized flowers)
Royal Saxe Germany (red)	Cupids
Royal Suhl Germany[16]	HI-1 (FD R)
	Mythological figures
ABK Royal Vienna[17]	Saxe FDa
	FD S

Endnotes

1. This mold number was assigned by Mary F. Gaston in *The Encyclopedia of R.S. Prussia*, Series 1 (AB Collector Books, 1984).
2. Capers mark RS 4.3(R)
3. This transfer is shown by R.H. Capers on p. 131 in *Capers Notes on the Marks of Prussia*, (Alphabet Printing, 1996).
4. Letters designate decoration patterns identified by Mary Gaston in *Encyclopedia of R.S. Prussia*, Series 4.
5. Capers mark RS 1.4R 3
6. The bent yellow rose dangles from a cluster.
7. Capers mark RS 5.3(G) 2
8. Capers mark RS 5.3R 18
9. There are actually two transfers in Saxe b as defined by M.F. Gaston in *Encyclopedia of R.S. Prussia* series 4. The term Saxe b-1 is used here for the open multicolored flowers, and b-2 for the red/pink roses. We also include both transfers under the decor HI 13 designation.
10. Capers mark RS 5.3R 20
11. Mythological figures in swing, holding lens, holding basket.
12. Capers mark RS 5.3R 21
13. Capers mark RS 5.3R 17
14. Victorian scenes, woman watering flowers, feeding chickens, with fan, with dog.
15. Capers mark RS 5.3R 5
16. Capers mark RS 5.3R 1
17. Capers mark RS 5.3R 22

Appendix 9
Royal Vienna in Bawo and Dotter Bulletins

The B & D Bulletin was apparently a short-lived journal, for the only issues in the Library of Congress were published from July 1898 to December 1899. Bawo and Dotter was a wholesale company in New York, NY, who carried china from many European firms. We reproduce several pages from various issues of their bulletin showing Royal Vienna, and "clever imitations" of Royal Vienna made by the firm of Erdmann Schlegelmilch. These "Vienna Luster Vases" are known to be marked with "Royal Saxe", crown, and "E.S." in blue green (Capers mark ES 3.4G 2). These products pre-date those made by Reinhold Schlegelmilch and marked with Royal Vienna Germany (red) made by Reinhold Schlegelmilch by at least two years.

Plate 716. Illustration of a 17" vase in the Jan. 16, 1899 Bawo & Dotter Bulletin. This vase was not stocked, as only import orders were taken. *Courtesy of Tom Felt.*

Plate 717. Illustration of "Vienna Lustre Vases" offered in the Sept. 1899 Bawo & Dotter Bulletin. The middle vase (in maroon with a heavy gold decoration around the central transfer) is illustrated (with trademark) by Capers (Capers, 1996).

Plate 718. Large lidded urn, assembled from two pieces, showing the two transfers used on the vases shown in Plate 714 and Plate 715.

Plate 719. Example of the Erdmann Schlegelmilch trademark used on the vase shown in Plate 716.

Index